MESSAGES FROM LUKE
Key stage 2 assembly outlines on Luke's gospel

Melanie Small

Copyright © Melanie Small 2003

First published 2003
ISBN 1 85999 715 5

Scripture Union, 207–209 Queensway, Bletchley, Milton Keynes, MK2 2EB, England.
Email: info@scriptureunion.org.uk
Website: www.scriptureunion.org.uk

Scripture Union Australia
Locked Bag 2, Central Coast Business Centre, NSW 2252
Website: www.su.org.au

Scripture Union USA
PO Box 987, Valley Forge, PA 19482
www.scriptureunion.org

All rights reserved. The activities and illustrations in this book may be photocopied for use. This permission is granted freely to owners of this book. This arrangement does not allow the printing of any of the published material in permanent form. Nor does it allow the printing of words or illustrations for resale or for any commercial use. Apart from this, no part of this publication may be reproduced, stored in a retrieval system, or transmitted in any form or by any means, electronic, mechanical, photocopying, recording or otherwise, without the prior permission of Scripture Union.

The right of Melanie Small to be identified as author of this work has been asserted by her in accordance with the Copyright, Designs and Patents Act 1988.

Scripture quotations are from the Contemporary English Version published by HarperCollins Publishers, copyright © 1991, 1992, 1995 American Bible Society, and from the *Holy Bible*, New Living Translation, copyright © 1996. Used by permission of Tyndale House Publishers, Inc., Wheaton, Illinois 60189. All rights reserved.

British Library Cataloguing-in-Publication Data.
A catalogue record of this book is available from the British Library.

Printed and bound in Malta by Interprint.

Cover design: Hurlock Design

Scripture Union is an international Christian charity working with churches in more than 130 countries, providing resources to bring the good news about Jesus Christ to children, young people and families and to encourage them to develop spiritually through the Bible and prayer.
As well as our network of volunteers, staff and associates who run holidays, church-based events and school Christian groups, we produce a wide range of publications and support those who use our resources through training programmes.

Contents page

Introduction

. 5

Theme index

. 8

Chronological index to Bible passages

. 9

Section 1: Get the message!

1 Message for Theophilus! 11
2 Message for Zechariah! 15
3 Message for Mary! 19
4 A message from long ago! 23
5 Message for some shepherds! .27

Section 2: What's Jesus all about?

1 An amazing identity 31
2 A family tree: Jesus the man 35
3 A job to do! 39
4 A strange twist 43
5 A warm welcome 47
6 An amazing gift from the King .51
7 An unbelievable event 57
8 An invisible helper 59

Section 3: Tell us a story!

1 The great feast . . . . . . *Luke 14* 61
2 The story of the lost son 65
3 The Pharisee and the tax collector 71
4 The story of the sower 75

Section 4: The power!

1 Power over circumstances 79
2 Power over life and death 83
3 Power over nature 87
4 Power over sin 91
5 Power to teach 95

Section 5: What do you think?

1 What did his friends think? 99
2 What did the businessman think? 103
3 What did the criminals think? .107
4 What did the fisherman think? 113
5 What did the follower think? .117
6 What did the officer think? 121
7 What did Mary think? 125

Introduction

Welcome to this collection of Christian assemblies for Key Stage 2 (Scottish primaries 4–7) pupils. This introduction should help you to get the most from the collection and explains how the different sections and assemblies fit together. It also gives a general guide to how each assembly is structured.

All the assemblies in the collection are based on the Gospel of Luke. Luke is one of the books of the Bible, the scripture of the Christian faith. It is one of the four accounts of the life of Jesus whom Christians believe was the Son of God. (The other three are the Gospels of Matthew, Mark and John.) As such, Luke is a key text in understanding the basis of Christianity.

This collection aims to help children learn about the historical figure of Jesus and the claims that the Bible makes about him through the stories in Luke's Gospel. The Gospel was written by a first-century doctor called Luke, who drew together a number of eyewitness accounts of the things that Jesus said and did.

All the assemblies involve significant pupil participation both in the introductory activity and often in telling the story itself. The collection is divided into thematic strands. These strands are reflected in the five sections into which this book is divided:

Section 1: Get the message!

Looking at the theme of the messages given to people in the first two chapters of Luke's Gospel, this section is designed to be used as a series of five assemblies and would be particularly suitable for the weeks leading up to Christmas.

Section 2: What's Jesus all about?

Designed to be used as a series, these assemblies give an overview of Jesus' life – who he claimed to be and what his purpose was. Taking up the story after the account of Jesus' birth, the eight assemblies span the whole of Luke's Gospel.

Section 3: Tell us a story!

Four separate assemblies based on parables from Luke's Gospel. As these are fictional stories Jesus told, it might be a good idea to use a large storybook as a visual illustration. Make it a feature of those assemblies that you open the storybook when you are beginning the fictional story.

Section 4: The power!

These five separate assemblies look at stories in Luke's Gospel which reveal different aspects of Jesus' power.

Section 5: What do you think?

Seven separate assemblies investigating different people's reactions to Jesus – what they thought of him and how he affected their lives.

While the first two sections are designed to be used as a series, each assembly could also stand alone. This may be particularly helpful at certain times of the year, for example, Christmas or Easter, or when dealing with particular themes. A thematic index is included on page 8. This index also cross-references assemblies from different sections which can be thematically grouped together. There is also a chronological index of passages from Luke's Gospel on page 9.

Pupil involvement is designed to be fun and should help the assemblies to come alive, while allowing the assembly-taker to retain control! Some of the assemblies involve a lot of pupil participation in telling the Bible story by way of drama and responses, whereas others only involve pupils in the introductory activity.

It should be noted that many of the original Bible stories have an 'all-male cast', and this has been preserved in the re-telling of the stories within this collection. However, there is no reason why girls should not take on the male roles, if they are happy to do so, or alternatively, a greater proportion of girls could take part in the introductory activities.

The assembly outlines in this collection all follow the same general format:

Title and Bible base: the passage and subject that the assembly deals with.

Teaching objectives: what does the assembly aim to teach?

You will need: the materials and resources you will need to get hold of before the assembly. These may include resources to be copied on to card or acetate. Generally these are included within the book as photocopiable resources.

When thinking about costumes, it is a good idea to keep them simple. For example, different hats can be enough to help the children to imagine the characters being depicted. Charity shops and jumble sales are a good source of cheap clothes – look out for dressing gowns or ornate pieces of fabric to make 'biblical' clothes!

Be wary of using very complicated costumes as these are likely to be time-consuming and may become more of a distraction. Remember, costumes are fun, but they are not essential!

Most other materials used in the assemblies should be easily found, but it is advisable to check in advance if there are materials you will need to buy.

Introductory activity: this is a light-hearted introduction to the theme of the assembly, and takes the form of a quiz or a challenge, involving either the whole assembly or a few volunteers at the front.

The main body of the assembly follows, in which the Bible stories are presented in a variety of different ways, using drama, responses and visual aids. The sections in italic type give directions for you, while sections in solid type are the assembly 'script'. The assemblies will work best, however, when you are comfortable enough with the content to carry the theme through without needing to follow the book word for word.

Optional prayer time: each assembly includes a suggestion for prayer to end the assembly, if this is appropriate in the particular setting in which it is being used.

The assembly outlines do not contain specific suggestions for music as it is recognised that not everyone is musical! However, songs could be added at the beginning or the end of each assembly. Most contemporary collections of children's songs suitable for assemblies have a thematic index to assist in choosing appropriate songs to accompany each assembly.

Theme index

Themes: linked assemblies (refer to Contents page)

Palm Sunday	2.5
Lent/Good Friday	2.6
Easter	2.7
Pentecost	2.8
Advent	1.2, 1.3, 1.4
Christmas	1.5
The Bible	1.1
Prayer	1.2, 4.5, 3.3
Forgiveness	4.4
Miracles	2.7, 4.1, 4.2, 4.3, 4.4, 5.4, 5.6
Baptism	2.1
Peter	5.4, 5.5

Chronological index to Bible passages

Luke 1:1–4	1.1
Luke 1:5–25	1.2
Luke 1:26–38	1.3
Luke 1:68–80	1.4
Luke 2:8–20	1.5
Luke 3:21,22	2.1
Luke 3:23–38	2.2
Luke 5:1–11	5.4
Luke 5:17–26	4.4
Luke 5:27–32	2.3
Luke 7:1–10	5.6
Luke 7:36–50	5.7
Luke 8:4–15	3.4
Luke 8:22–25	4.3
Luke 8:40–56	4.2
Luke 9:10–17	4.1
Luke 9:18–20	5.5
Luke 10:38–42	5.1
Luke 11:1–13	4.5
Luke 14:15–24	3.1
Luke 15:11–32	3.2
Luke 18:9–14	3.3
Luke 19:1–10	5.2
Luke 19:28–40	2.5
Luke 22:7–30	2.4
Luke 23:1–25	2.6
Luke 23:32–43	5.3
Luke 24:1–12	2.7
Luke 24:36–53	2.8

Message for Theophilus!

1.1

Bible base: Luke 1:1–4

Teaching objectives:

To introduce the Christian belief that Luke's Gospel is a true record of Jesus' life.

> **You will need:**
> - Two large sheets of paper.
> - Two marker pens.
> - A copy of Luke's Gospel.
> - The words 'What God has done' photocopied on to acetate or a large piece of paper.
>
> *Optional:*
> - Celebrity magazine.
> - Luke 1:1–4 photocopied on to acetate.

Introductory activity:

Imagine meeting a famous person and chatting with them! Who would you want to meet? (*You may wish to have a copy of a celebrity magazine with you to give examples of some of the people they could meet.*)

Take some of the pupils' suggestions, and choose two who have chosen very different people to come to the front. (Make sure that you choose two pupils who can write clearly; ask members of staff to help if in doubt. It would also be advisable to choose older pupils.) Explain to the chosen pupils that they are going to write a letter to someone to tell them about their celebrity encounter.

Give each pupil one of the sheets of paper and a marker pen, and place them at either side of the assembly hall (the rest won't see it until it's read out).

Ask them to write down the following pieces of information in big letters After writing each item, they should fold the paper down so that the words are hidden and then swap sheets with the other pupil before adding the next bit of information, like a game of 'consequences'. (You may wish to have prepared two sheets in advance, in the form of a letter, with the pupils merely filling in gaps, which will keep the activity moving quickly.)

They should write down the following information:

- Who they are writing to (eg 'Dear Mum, Dad, Granny')
- Who they meet (eg a film star, a pop star, royalty)
- What they say to the celebrity
- What the celebrity says to them
- What the result is

As they are doing this, ask the assembly to think of who they would put in the story if they were writing it.

Read out the 'letters' which are created, adding in the necessary words to make full sentences. They may be either funny or nonsensical: comment accordingly.

The letters are jumbled because they are a mixture of two different accounts written about imaginary encounters with two very different people. Neither of the pupils has actually met their celebrity, so their accounts do not really help us get to know this person better.

Choose one of the celebrities and ask the pupils how they would find out more information about what this person is like. Possible suggestions: Internet, magazines, newspaper articles, interviewing people who know them, etc.

Two thousand years ago a man called Luke wanted to write a letter to his friend Theophilus about Jesus. How could he have found out more about Jesus? Without the Internet or international media sources, Luke went to the most accurate source of information – people who knew Jesus, or had met him and had seen what he had done in his life. Once Luke had gathered all the information, he wrote it all down in a long letter to Theophilus. *(If you have an acetate of the opening verses of Luke's Gospel, show it to the assembly now, explaining that this is how Luke begins his letter.) Show the pupils a copy of Luke's Gospel.*

This is a copy of the letter that Luke wrote to his friend. Imagine if Luke had not written it all down, but had just told Theophilus all that he had discovered: we might never have heard all the stories that are recorded in this part of the Bible.

The New Living Translation of the Bible refers to the eyewitnesses' reports of 'what God has done'. *Show these words to the assembly.* Christians believe that Luke's story, and the whole Bible, is the story of 'what God has done'.

> **Optional prayer time:**
>
> Thank God that Luke did write all his stories down, so that we can read them too and learn more about Jesus.

Message for Zechariah!

1.2

Bible base: Luke 1:5–25

Teaching objectives:

To show that Christians believe God answers prayers. Sometimes the answer is unbelievable, but they believe he can be trusted.

> **You will need:**
> - Chewy fruit sweets which are sold in tightly-wrapped paper.
> - Clothes to dress up two pupils – one boy and one girl – as old people, eg a tweed jacket, a shawl, an old-fashioned handbag, etc.
> - Two envelopes addressed to Zechariah, with 'God' written on the back as the sender's name. One envelope should contain the words 'Your wife, Elizabeth, will have a son' and the other the words, 'He will persuade people to turn to God and will prepare the way for God's Son.'

Introductory activity:

If you are doing this assembly as part of a series before Christmas, ask the pupils what presents they are hoping to receive. Alternatively, at other times in the year, ask if anyone has a birthday coming up. Ask them to raise their hand if they want to tell you about the presents they would like to receive.

Ask three pupils to come to the front of the assembly hall. Ask them if they are right or left-handed. Put a chewy fruit sweet wrapped in paper in their other hand and ask them to unwrap it using only that hand. Encourage the rest of the pupils to cheer them on.

When they have finished, ask them why they kept trying to get the sweet opened. It is because they wanted to eat it. If they didn't care, they would have given up.

Today's story is about a man called Zechariah and his wife Elizabeth. Just like our volunteers, there was something that they really wanted. It wasn't just a sweet however, and they had wanted this thing for many years.

Choose a boy and a girl to come to the front to be Zechariah and Elizabeth. Start to dress them up in costumes as you build up a picture of what they were like.

Zechariah and Elizabeth lived a long time ago in a hot country a long way from here, but to help us imagine them more easily, we will dress them up in modern clothes. They were also very old – older than your grandparents – so we will dress them up to look like older people.

Zechariah and Elizabeth had lived a long and good life, and had been very happy. But one thing in their life made them very sad: they had no children. They both loved children, but they had never had any of their own. Now they were so old, there was no chance they could have a child. This was the only thing in their life that really made them sad. *Encourage the pupils at the front to look sad.*

The Bible says that Zechariah and Elizabeth loved God very much and had always tried to obey him in everything they did. Because they loved him so much and believed that he loved them even more, they used to talk to him all the time about everything they were thinking and feeling.

They believed that God was very powerful and that he was the only one who could help them. Every day they would tell him about how much they wanted a child.

Zechariah was a priest, and one day he was in the temple on his own, praying to God, when something amazing happened: an angel appeared! Zechariah was very afraid, but the angel told him not to be. He was sent from God to give Zechariah a message.

Give one of the envelopes addressed to 'Zechariah' to your volunteer. Ask them to open it and read what it says:

'Your wife, Elizabeth, will have a son.'

At last, here was an answer to their prayers! But that was not the end of the message.

Give the pupil the second envelope to read out:

'He will persuade people to turn to God and will prepare the way for God's Son.'

God had heard their prayers and had answered them, but his answer was even better than they had imagined. Not only would Elizabeth have a baby, but this baby would have a very special job, preparing people for God's Son, Jesus.

The message was so amazing that Zechariah found it very hard to believe. Elizabeth was so old! But Elizabeth believed the message for one simple reason.

Ask 'Elizabeth' to check on the back of the envelope to see who the message is from and tell the rest of the assembly.

Elizabeth knew they could trust this message because it was from someone they knew: God. She knew that God loved them and wouldn't lie to them. Now God had answered their prayer in an amazing way!

Luke's Gospel is an exciting message to Theophilus *(only mention Theophilus if you have already done the previous assembly)* and to us, but this is the first exciting message within his story. Christians believe it is a message that shows us that God is in touch with people and answers their prayers in more incredible ways than they could ever imagine. Elizabeth's son was John the Baptist, sent to prepare people for an even more exciting message still to come.

> **Optional prayer time:**
>
> Give thanks that God heard Zechariah and Elizabeth's prayers and answered them. Thank him that he is still in touch with people today.

Message for Mary!

1.3

Bible base: Luke 1:26–38

Teaching objectives:

To show that Christians believe God can have surprising things to say to anyone, not just important people.

You will need:

- Twenty-one cards with the following options written on them: Mary, Bob, Joseph; In her teens, In her twenties, In her thirties; In Jerusalem, In London, In a tiny village; The king, An angel, A ghost; God, The king, Another angel; You will be a famous singer, You will marry the king, You will have a baby; The baby would be God's Son Jesus, The baby would be a great leader, The baby would be King for ever.

Introductory activity:

Run the following multiple-choice quiz either with the whole assembly or with a few volunteers at the front. (The correct answer is in capitals.)

1. How long did the 100 years war last?
a) 100 years
b) 200 years
c) 116 YEARS

2. What country do panama hats come from?
a) ECUADOR
b) Panama
c) United States

3. In what month do Russians celebrate the October Revolution?
a) October
b) NOVEMBER (the Russian calendar is 13 days behind ours)
c) January

4. What is a camelhair brush made of?
a) Human hair
b) Camel hair
c) SQUIRREL FUR

5. What creature are the Canary Islands named after?
a) DOGS (from Latin)
b) Canaries
c) Goldfish

6. What was King George VI's first name?
a) Gerald
b) ALBERT
c) George

7. Where are Chinese gooseberries from?
a) China
b) NEW ZEALAND
c) Malaysia

8. How long did the 30 years war last?
a) 30 YEARS!
b) 35 years
c) 30 days

Find out how highly the pupils have scored. There were a lot of surprises in that quiz. Even the last answer was a surprise because we started to expect that the obvious one was wrong!

Today's story involves quite a few surprises too.

Include the following paragraph if you are doing this assembly following on from 'A message for Zechariah!':

Do you remember what Zechariah and Elizabeth, the old couple in the last assembly, were praying for? They really wanted a child, and God eventually answered their prayers when an angel came to tell them that they would have a very special son, who would prepare the way for God's Son. The young girl in today's story was definitely not praying for a child! She was surprised by what God chose to say to her.

We are going to build up a picture of what this person was like and then together work out the story of what happened to her. *Choose three volunteers to come to the front to help you to hold up cards that will tell the story.*

Firstly, we need to find out what this mystery person's name was. *Give each of the three pupils one of the following three names to hold up: Mary, Bob, Joseph.*

Pupils should vote for which they think is the right answer. Explain that you have already given them a clue! (ie you referred to 'her'). Tell them the correct answer and display the name 'Mary' at the front of the assembly hall.

Follow a similar pattern for the following facts. The correct answer is underlined in each case:

What age was she? *In her teens*, In her twenties, In her thirties
Where did she live? *In Jerusalem, In London, In a tiny village*

Mary was not an important person – probably no one outside her village even knew she existed! So, you can imagine her surprise when someone quite unexpected came to see her one day! Who do you think it was?

Give them the following three choices: The king, An angel, A ghost

When they have guessed, tell them the correct answer and display it at the front.

What a surprise! Mary was very worried when an angel appeared before her! But the angel reassured Mary and told her not to be afraid. He said that someone more important and amazing than him was very pleased with her and wanted to give her a message. Who do you think this was?

Give them the following three choices: God, The king, another angel. When they have guessed, tell them the correct answer and display it at the front.

Mary was not expecting a message from God! She probably didn't think that a young girl like her living in a little village was important enough for God to speak to. But God knew all about her and had a special job that only she could do.

So, what was the message? It seems quite ordinary at first, but actually it might be the most amazing message that anyone has ever received. Can you guess – or do you know – what that message was?

Give them the following three choices:
You will be a famous singer
You will marry the king
<u>You will have a baby</u>

When they have guessed, tell them the correct answer and display it at the front.

Mary was going to have a baby! But this would be no ordinary baby – he was someone very special indeed. You may have guessed already who it was.

Give them the following three choices:
<u>The baby would be God's Son, Jesus</u>
<u>The baby would be a great leader</u>
<u>The baby would be King for ever</u>

This was a trick – all three answers are right! Mary's baby would be Jesus, God's own Son. But the angel also said that because Jesus was God's Son, he would lead the people and would be King for ever.

Mary was just an ordinary young girl when God asked her to do a very important task for him. Mary said 'yes' because she trusted God and wanted to do what he said.

The Bible says that no one is too ordinary for God to be interested in them. Christians believe he has things that he wants to tell each person and things that he wants only them to do.

> **Optional prayer time:**
>
> Say thank you that God knows everything about each person's life. He is interested in them, no matter how unimportant they feel.

A message from long ago!

Bible base: Luke 1:68–80; Isaiah 9:6,7

Teaching objectives:

To discover that the message that Jesus was coming from God was sent to people long before his birth.

You will need:

- 'Text words' on acetate or card.
- A mobile phone with the text message 'A child is born! He will rule for ever from the throne of his ancestor David.' Set the phone to send the message to its own number when you press the 'send' button. Alternatively, write the words out as a letter in an envelope.
- A sign saying 'Isaiah' to hang around a pupil's neck.

Introductory activity:

Show the pupils the following 'texts'. Are they able to translate them?

XLnt	*excellent*
Pls	*please*
CuL8r	*see you later*
Pcm	*please call me*
LOL	*lots of love or laugh out loud*
Bfn	*bye for now*
Mbrsd	*embarrassed*

Today we are used to receiving messages from people almost immediately, thanks to email, text messages, telephones, etc.

God has been sending people messages for thousands of years, but sometimes we have to wait a long time to see exactly what God means by his messages.

Imagine we are now in the year 700 BC; that's 2,700 years ago! Let's meet a man who lived then, called Isaiah.

Choose a volunteer and put a sign saying 'Isaiah' around their neck. Choose about ten other children to come to the front at this point too; you will explain their role a little later.

About 2,700 years ago, the Bible says that God sent a message to Isaiah – you can still read the message in the Bible. Today we're going to imagine the message coming through in a form we are familiar with.

Press the 'send' button on your mobile phone, or ask the first person in the line to open the envelope.

Give the phone to 'Isaiah' to read out the message to the assembly. Encourage the pupil to pretend to be excited.

Isaiah was very excited about this news when he got it. But then he got older and older and still this promised ruler had not appeared. Imagine that this line of pupils is a long line of different generations of one family. Before Isaiah died, he passed the news on to his son, so that when God's promise happened on earth he would see and understand.

Ask 'Isaiah' to tell the message to the next pupil in a loud voice and pass them the phone.

Isaiah's son was very excited too, but then, many years later, when he too was an old man and the promised ruler had still not appeared, he told his daughter/son so that the message would not be forgotten.

The next pupil should pass the message along the line.

Continue to explain about the message being passed on through all the 'generations', asking the pupils to pass it on as you do so, until the last person has received the message and the mobile phone. Check that the message is still correct.

The people had to wait a very long time to see God's message come true. In fact, the people who first heard the message had been dead for hundreds of years before anything happened. Christians believe that God had sent messages to other people years before too, which gave details about what this baby would be like; for example, which family he would be part of and where he would be born.

So when, eventually, a baby was born in the right place from the right family and when some amazing things happened around the time of his birth, people remembered the things that Isaiah and the others had passed down to them. They believed that this was going to be a very special baby indeed!

> **Optional prayer time:**
>
> Say thank you to God for people like Isaiah who faithfully wrote down what they heard from God, to prepare people for the arrival of his Son. Thank him that we can still read these messages for ourselves in the Bible.

Message for some shepherds!

1.5

Bible base: Luke 2:8–20

Teaching objectives:

To explore how Christians believe the announcement of Jesus' birth to the shepherds shows that it is a message for everyone.

> **You will need:**
> - Pictures of scientists, shepherds and politicians from page 30 enlarged and photocopied on to acetate or card.
> - Six headlines from page 30 enlarged and photocopied on to separate acetates or strips of card.

Introductory activity:

Show the assembly the pictures of the three groups of people. Ask what job they think each group does. Explain that the first group are scientists, the second are shepherds and the third are politicians.

Show the assembly each of the first five headlines in turn. Which of our three groups should be the first to hear this news? Put the headline underneath the appropriate picture.

1. New discovery to save lives
2. New ruler in the nation
3. Important news from the King
4. New way to improve life
5. New sheep herding method discovered

The shepherds would be last to hear all the world-changing news – they might have heard about the new ways to herd sheep if they could be found on the hills! The shepherds we are going to look at today lived 2,000 years ago, before there were radios or newspapers, so they would have heard virtually nothing of what was happening even in their own country.

Christians believe that one night these shepherds heard the greatest news that anyone had ever heard. There had been about 700 years since God gave the message to Isaiah. *(Only mention if you have done the previous assembly on Isaiah.)* On this night, these shepherds were given a world exclusive!

If you are doing this assembly as part of the series 'Get the message!', ask if anyone can remember the message that Isaiah got from God in the last assembly. ('A child is born! He will rule for ever from the throne of his ancestor David.')

Look at all the headlines the other groups have. Christians believe that all these headlines came true the night that Jesus was born: he came to save lives; he came to be a ruler; he was sent from God, the King; and he would improve the life of his people. But, the amazing thing was that the first people to hear this message were not the scientists of the time *(take their headlines away)*, nor the politicians *(take their headlines away)*, but the shepherds *(put all the headlines with the shepherds)*.

These shepherds were all out in the fields, watching their sheep, minding their own business, when suddenly an angel appeared to them and told them that the person God had promised years before, whom they had heard about from their parents and grandparents, had finally been born in Bethlehem. And what was more, they were the first to hear about it! I wonder if they had ever been first to hear any news before?

So, why did they hear it first? The answer is in what the angel says. *Show them the final headline:*

6. 'I have good news for you, which will make everyone happy.'

The message of Jesus is not just for very clever or important people, but for everyone. Because of this, God made sure that the shepherds, who were not rich, important or even well thought of, heard it first. Christians believe that everyone is important to God and that he wants everyone to know about his Son, Jesus.

Optional prayer time:

Show all the headlines (apart from the one about sheep herding!) and pray through them, giving thanks that Jesus is the fulfilment of all these things.

New discovery to save lives.
New ruler in the nation.
Important news from the king.
New way to improve life.
New sheep herding method discovered.
'I have good news for you, which will make everyone happy.'

An amazing identity

2.1

―――――― *Bible base: Luke 3:21,22* ――――――

Teaching objectives:

To show pupils that the Bible claims Jesus is the Son of God.

> **You will need:**
> - Six pieces of card, each with two words of the following sentence written on them: 'You are my own dear Son, and I am pleased with you.' Luke 3:22. (Alternatively, use three or four balloons containing bits of the phrase.)
> *Optional:*
> - A copy of *Shrek* on video or DVD, cued for the scene where Donkey discovers Princess Fiona's secret. (1 hour, 26 seconds when Donkey says 'All right, all right, it's not that bad…' to 1 hour, 1 minute, 53 seconds when Fiona says, 'Don't you see Donkey, that's just the way it has to be.')
> - A celebrity quiz (see next page).

Introductory activity:

Have you ever overheard something important? What are the dangers of overhearing part of a conversation?

Either:

Show the clip from Shrek, *when Shrek overhears Princess Fiona talking to Donkey. Princess Fiona is explaining to Donkey that she turns into an ogre when the sun goes down. She doesn't want Shrek*

31

to know as he wouldn't like her. When Shrek overhears her saying 'Who could ever love a beast so hideous and ugly? Princess and ugly don't go together', Shrek thinks she is describing him.

What did Shrek think Princess Fiona was saying? What was she actually saying?

Princess Fiona did not want to be overheard, because she was hiding her real identity as an ogre.

Or:

Run a quiz in which snippets of information are given about various celebrities, with the pupils trying to guess who it is. Have five clues for each celebrity. Divide the assembly into two teams. If a pupil guesses the person's identity after one clue they receive five points for their team, down to one point if it takes all five clues.

Ideas for celebrities: a football player, a pop star, the Prime Minister, a member of the royal family, a soap opera character.

In today's story, God had a message for Jesus about how much he loved him, and he wanted everyone to hear it. He wanted to give people more than just a clue about what he was saying!

The Bible says that it all happened on the day that Jesus and lots of other people were being baptised. 'Being baptised' simply means that they were publicly saying that they wanted to follow God, and they did this by washing in a river and showing that they had a 'clean start' with God.

As Jesus was baptised, God had a message for him. It was an important message about who Jesus was and how God felt about him, but he wanted everyone, not just Jesus, to hear it. So, instead of whispering the message to Jesus, everyone heard a loud voice coming from heaven. What the voice said is written on the cards (or balloons).

Bring six pupils to the front and give them a piece of card at random. Ask them to stand in a line and take it in turns to read out the words on their card.

The words are in the wrong order, so it doesn't make sense. Can we work out what the voice actually said? *Sort the words into the right order.*

'You are my own dear Son, and I am pleased with you.' Luke 3:22.

Encourage the pupils to read the words aloud with you, to hear what God said to Jesus.

A voice from heaven would definitely have attracted people's attention! In *Shrek*, Princess Fiona did not want to be overheard. Most of us would not want to be overheard when we are talking about a person we love. But Christians believe that God wanted everyone to hear him say who Jesus was and how much he loved him.

Christians believe that God still wants people to know who Jesus is, and the verse on these cards tells us what the Bible says about who he is. The loud voice from heaven must have been a surprise and must have made people listen carefully.

> **Optional prayer time:**
>
> Pray that God would help us understand more about Jesus and who he is. Thank God that we were allowed to listen in on this conversation between him and Jesus!

A family tree: Jesus the man

2.2

Bible base: Luke 3:23–38

Teaching objectives:

To show that Jesus was a real man who knew what it was like to grow up in a family.

> **You will need (*optional*):**
> - An acetate of Luke 3:23–38.

Introductory activity:

Begin with the following quiz about families, either bringing some volunteers to the front or dividing the assembly into two teams.

1. What is the name for your mum's mum? *grandmother*
2. What is the name for your dad's brother? *uncle*
3. What is the name for your mum's brother? *uncle*
4. What relation is your mum's sister's child to you? *cousin*
5. If your sister had a baby, what relation would she be to you? *niece*
6. What does the word 'siblings' mean? *brothers and sisters*

Families may be quite different now to what they were like many years ago, but people have always been part of families. Sometimes it is easy to forget that famous people you read about in history were also normal people in normal families *(you may wish to give a few examples of people whom the pupils might be studying in history, or some current celebrity examples)*.

Do one of the following activities. Either:

Ask about six pupils to come to the front. Ask them to cross their arms in front of them and join hands with the people either side of them. Once pupils are 'linked up', ask them to mime the following actions:

Brush your teeth
Comb your hair
Eat some breakfast cereal
Blow your nose
Tie your shoelace

Keep this activity fast moving to avoid it getting out of control. Ask the pupils to take their seats.

It can be difficult being part of a family. Sometimes we are all trying to do the same thing at the same time and we get in each other's way!

Or:

Jesus, too, was part of a family. When I read out the following statements about his family, raise your hand if you think that it is something which the Bible says is true.

1. Jesus had brothers and sisters. (true)
2. Jesus had grandchildren. (false; he had no children, and so no grandchildren)
3. Jesus had a cousin called John. (true)
4. Jesus was an uncle. (probably true, if his brothers and sisters had children)
5. Jesus' mum was called Martha. (false; she was called Mary)
6. Jesus was the eldest in his family. (true)
7. Jesus' dad was a tax collector. (false; he was a carpenter)

Christians believe that Jesus led an amazing life, *and in the coming weeks we will be discovering some of the things that he did (include if you are doing this assembly as part of a series)*. You may have heard of some of the famous events in his life, like when he turned water into wine, or brought a little girl back to life, or fed 5,000 people. When you hear of amazing things like this, it is easy to imagine that Jesus was just an imaginary superhero who flew to the rescue whenever things went wrong, but that's not what he was like. Jesus did have amazing powers, but he was also a human being, a member of a normal family with brothers and sisters, aunts and uncles.

The Bible makes this clear when it names people in Jesus' family tree. It's quite an impressive list!

Ask the pupils to raise their hand if they know their mum or dad's first name. Ask them to keep their hand raised if they know their grandfather or grandmother's name. Ask them to keep their hand raised if they know their great-grandfather's or great-grandmother's name.

By this stage there should be very few hands remaining!

The Bible lists 77 names in Jesus' family tree! *Show the acetate of Luke 3:23–38 at this point if you are using it.* There can be no doubt that Jesus was a real human being in a real family.

Do you ever find it hard, living with your family? Families argue over lots of things, and sometimes we feel that no one in our family really understands us. Christians believe that Jesus can help us when we tell him about problems we face, because he is God. He was also a human being so he can understand what it is like to be part of a family.

> **Optional prayer time:**
>
> Say thank you to God for the family that we have and the people we live with. Thank him that he can understand what it is like to be part of a family.

A job to do!

2.3

———— *Bible base: Luke 5:27–32* ————

Teaching objectives:

To show that Christians believe Jesus came to do a very specific job on earth: to ask people to turn away from doing wrong things and follow him.

> **You will need:**
> - Cards with the following good things written on them: lots of money; a good job; a big car; friends and family; happiness; peace; lots of chocolate.
> - A packet of sticky plasters.
> - Fine clothes to dress 'Levi'.
> - 'Healthy people don't need a doctor, but sick people do' written on acetate or card.

Introductory activity:

Choose two or three volunteers to come to the front. Show them the cards with all the 'good things' written on them. If they could only have three things in life, which three would it be?

Once they have chosen three, ask them to reduce it to two, and finally, if they could choose only one thing, what would it be?

There are lots of things which we would like to have in life, but while a nice car and a big house might be fun, life would be pretty miserable if you had these things but no one to share them with. Human beings need to have other people around them, and for most people, friends and/or family will be the most important things in their life.

The person we are going to meet in today's story had lots of things in life. His name was Levi.

Choose a pupil to be Levi.

The Bible says Levi was very wealthy and so was always very well dressed (*dress up 'Levi' in fine clothes*). But although Levi looked good, he was not very happy as he did not have any friends.

Levi was Jewish, as were all the other people who lived in his town, but Levi worked for the Romans. The Romans had taken over the town and made the Jewish people pay huge taxes to them, so people really didn't like them very much. Levi's job was to gather in these Roman taxes from his people, the Jews. Often he would gather in more money than people owed and keep the rest for himself. As you can imagine, Levi was very unpopular!

So, while Levi was very well dressed on the outside, the reality was that he was not a very nice person on the inside. There were lots of things wrong in his life, such as greed and selfishness – what the Bible calls 'sin'. The Bible describes sin as a sickness, so to help us remember that Levi is not as fine as he would like to appear on the outside, we'll give Levi some plasters to cover up his sin! *Stick plasters over Levi's fine clothes.*

One day, as Levi was walking along on his own, as usual, an amazing thing happened. Levi had got used to being ignored by everyone he met, but suddenly, from the middle of a big crowd, a man came towards him.

And even more amazingly, the man actually spoke to him! What do you think he said?

Take suggestions from the assembly. Pupils may suggest that the man would ask Levi why he had plasters all over his clothes, or would tell him he looked stupid. Remind the pupils that the plasters represent sin – bad things that Levi had done or thought – so the man might have asked him why he was so bad or so mean.

Actually, what he said was this:

'Come and be my follower!'

The man who came to speak to Levi was Jesus. Levi must have been so surprised that this man whom everybody wanted to be near had asked him, unpopular and sinful Levi, to be his follower! What Levi wanted more than anything was friends and here was

Jesus asking him to come and be his friend. Levi was so happy that the first thing he did was throw a party so that everyone else could come and meet Jesus.

When people criticised Jesus for being friends with someone like Levi, he said a very strange thing.

Show them the acetate or card with the words:

'Healthy people don't need a doctor, but sick people do.'

What do you think he meant? Look at our Levi for a clue!

The Bible teaches that Jesus came to ask people who were needy to be friends with God, not people who thought they were already good enough. Jesus came to help people who wanted to be better people on the inside, not just on the outside.

Start to take the plasters off Levi's clothes.

Christians believe that Jesus helped Levi to do this, and this is what the Bible says Jesus can do for people today too. Christians believe that this was why Jesus came to earth: to help people to turn from the bad things they do and follow him.

> **Optional prayer time:**
>
> Give thanks that Jesus cares about all the things that are wrong inside us and that his reason for coming to earth was to help people, not to make their life harder.

A strange twist

2.4

Bible base: Luke 22:7–30

Teaching objectives:

To show that Christians believe Jesus' death was part of God's plan.

> **You will need:**
> - The words 'I must die because it is part of God's plan' written in sections on separate pieces of card.
> - 'Twisted tale' visual aid from page 45, copied on to a large piece of paper that will be visible to the assembly.

Introductory activity:

Bring about twelve pupils to the front and get them to stand in two circles of six facing inwards. Ask them all to stretch their arms out in front of them and then take hold of two hands at random. The two groups should then race to untangle themselves without letting go of each other's hands.

Everyone's arms were twisted together and it took a while to untangle them! Today's story has a twist in it, and it might take a while to work out how to untangle it.

The story takes place when Jesus is in Jerusalem, where King Herod rules. Herod was unpopular, but a lot of people really liked Jesus because he helped them and cared for them. When he arrived in Jerusalem, the people greeted him as a king.

The Bible says that Jesus was coming to Jerusalem to be their king, but the story wasn't as simple as they perhaps thought! Jesus would be King one day, but he wasn't going to go to King Herod's palace and overthrow him as the people might have expected. Our story takes place one night, when Jesus was having a meal with his followers and began to reveal his secret plans to them. Can you read what the plan was? Unscramble the words to find out.

Arrange the words on cards at the front, making sure that the order is muddled up.

The plan was twisted up so that we could not read it at first – it was not obvious. And as a plan, it's not a very obvious way to become King either. What a strange twist! It seems like a strange idea, to plan to die, but this was actually Jesus' winning idea. Long before they had gone to Jerusalem, and long before this meal they were now sharing, Jesus had told them that this was God's plan for him.

Hold up the unfolded large 'twisted tale' sheet.

This is an outline of God's plan. It doesn't look very clear, but that is because there are a few twists in the tale.

Fold the paper along the lines so that what the assembly can see are the words 'Jesus will be King'.

Jesus will be King, just as the people hoped, but *(flip the paper over so that it says 'Jesus will be killed')* before he becomes King, he will be killed.

How could he be killed and then become King? There is another twist to the tale!

Lift the flap at 'A' to reveal the words 'Jesus will come back to life'.

Jesus would come back to life! And then, when he had overcome death, he would be King in God's kingdom *(lift flap at 'B' so that the sentence 'Jesus will be King' is revealed)*.

We are back at the sentence we started with, 'Jesus will be King'. But there were amazing twists in the tale, which meant that Jesus was going to be a special King like no other. The Bible says that Jesus would die and would then become King in God's kingdom for ever.

> **Optional prayer time:**
>
> Pray that God would help us to understand the twists in the amazing story of Jesus' life and death.

Jesus will come back to life

be king

Jesus will be killed

Fold ①
Fold ②
A
B

A warm welcome

2.5

Bible base: Luke 19:28–40

Teaching objectives:

To show that people believed Jesus was a king. But he was a different sort of king. His power was far, far greater than anything people had known (this will become more apparent in subsequent assemblies. If using as a one-off then this will need to be explained!).

> **You will need:**
> - A cardboard crown for the winner of the quiz.
> - Some gold or red fabric to turn a chair into a throne.
> - A velvet dressing gown or red or gold fabric to look like a king's robe.
> - Large leaves made out of green tissue paper.

Introductory activity:

Choose four pupils to come to the front and take part in a royal quiz. The winner will be crowned king or queen of the primary school you are in.

1. Where does the king or queen of Great Britain live? *Buckingham Palace*
2. What does the king or queen wear on their head on special occasions? *A crown*
3. Who is Prince William's brother? *Prince Harry*
4. Who is Queen Elizabeth II's husband? *Prince Philip*
5. How many years has Queen Elizabeth reigned in Great Britain? *(NB 2002 was her 50th year on the throne)*
6. Who is next in line to the throne? *Prince Charles*

7. When was the Golden Jubilee? *2002*
8. Does every country have a king or queen? *No*

When you have a winner for the quiz, ask them to stay at the front of the assembly. Then proceed to ask the pupils how we could make them look more like a king or queen. Start to dress them up as a king/queen:

Put the crown on their head.
Cover a chair with material to pretend it is a throne.
Dress them in a robe.

Ask the pupils to imagine that the assembly hall is actually a very grand palace.

Ask them questions about what they think a king or queen does. How would they travel around? Where would their palace be?

Make the point that in our country, the king or queen does not have very much power any more, but in some countries, and years ago in Britain, the monarch ruled the country. They had the power to make people's lives better or worse! You may choose to make reference to a film that the children would know that shows a king who has real power, for example, The Lion King *or the pharaoh in* Prince of Egypt. *If you have time, you could show a clip.*

In today's story, we meet someone whom the people treated like a king, but he was not like the sort of king we have just described.
    He did not have a crown *(remove the crown)*. He did not have a fine throne to s t on *(take the fabric off the seat)*. He did not have a fine palace to live in. He did not have fine robes *(remove the robes)*. In fact, he had none of the things we have imagined a king should have. He didn't have a carriage and he didn't live in the capital city.
    However, people thought he was a king because of the things he did. Do you remember that we said that in other countries, and in the old days, kings and queens had lots of power? People thought this man was a king because of the amazing things he did to help them.
    Have you guessed who it is yet? This person was Jesus. The Bible says that people had seen the amazing miracles that Jesus did and the way he had made people's lives better. He wasn't a king sitting on a throne, with robes and a crown *(draw their attention again to the robes and crown that you have taken off your king or queen)*. They believed that he was a different sort of king, sent from God to help them.

Jesus was coming into the capital city on a donkey rather than in a carriage. The people didn't go to find him in a palace, they came out on to the streets and shouted and cheered as he went by. They threw palm branches and cloaks on the ground to make a carpet for him, praising God for the amazing things they had seen him do.

Throw the tissue paper leaves and the material used for the king's cloak and throne on to the ground and ask your 'king' or 'queen' to walk over them.

Something about Jesus made people believe that he was very special – special enough to be a king, even though he didn't have the crown or the palace or any of the other things we associate with kings.

The Bible says that Jesus was a King. *Put the crown back on the pupil's head.* Rather than being the king who is in charge of a country like our king or queen, he is a King who is in charge of people's lives. Christians are people who believe that Jesus was someone so special that they want him to be in charge of their lives – like a king!

> **Optional prayer time:**
>
> Thank God that Jesus really cared about people and can make a difference.

An amazing gift from the King

2.6

Bible base: Luke 23:1–25

Teaching objectives:

To show that the Bible says Jesus' death was the punishment for other people's guilt.

> **You will need:**
> - A bottle of water, a jumper and a loaf of bread, each individually wrapped as though they are presents. Do not try to disguise the shape of the items.
> - Prompt cards to show the assembly saying 'Give us Barabbas!', 'Kill him!' and 'You're free!'
> - Pictures from pages 55 and 56 photocopied on to acetate or card.

Introductory activity:

Show the assembly the three presents that you have wrapped up. Choose one pupil to come to the front to have a closer look, but do not let them unwrap them. Ask them to imagine the following situations: which present would they want most in each one?

    You are really hungry
    You are really thirsty
    You are really cold

Unwrap the presents to discover if the pupil made the right choice. Ask the pupil to sit down again.

Today's story is about a man who received an amazing gift, which was what he wanted more than anything else. Unlike the presents we have here, it was not something that could be wrapped up. The man's name was Barabbas.

The Bible doesn't tell us an awful lot about Barabbas, but what we do know is that he started a riot and murdered someone. And he doesn't look very happy, because he was caught. He was found guilty and put in prison. *Show picture 1a.*

We can imagine Barabbas feeling very lonely, sitting in a prison cell on his own and feeling very sorry for himself. With no one else to talk to, perhaps Barabbas started to think about how stupid he had been. He knew that the punishment for his crime was the death penalty. Why had he done it?

Jesus was also in prison, because the people had accused him of causing trouble and saying things that weren't true. But, unlike Barabbas, Jesus hadn't done anything wrong. *Show picture 1b.*

I wonder what Barabbas was thinking.

Perhaps as he thought about the punishment that was waiting for him, he realised that he deserved it. He knew that what he had been doing was wrong, and now he had been caught out, he knew that he deserved the punishment. Barabbas was miserable.

Ask the pupils what gift Barabbas would want more than anything else at this moment.

More than anything, Barabbas wanted to be free. Perhaps one day, as Barabbas was sitting in his cell, he heard crowds outside the prison shouting something over and over again. What was it? He couldn't make out the words at first, but as he listened, it seemed to get louder and louder, as though the people were getting closer. Eventually, he could hear what it was they were saying:

Hold up the prompt card 'Give us Barabbas!' and encourage the assembly to shout it over and over.

Barabbas was going to be released! The people were calling for him!

But then, just as he was getting excited, he heard their shouts change to something much less pleasant:

Hold up the prompt card 'Kill him!' and encourage the assembly to shout it over and over.

Maybe it was not so good after all. Now it seemed as if the people were calling for his execution.

Barabbas was suddenly very scared. And he became more and more scared as he heard the heavy footsteps of the jailer coming along the corridor *(you could add some atmosphere by walking heavily across the assembly hall)*. And then he could hear the rattle of the jailer's keys and the locking and unlocking of doors. Barabbas had never been so scared in his life, as he realised that this could be the end.

Suddenly, the doors swung open and the jailer appeared in the doorway, and in his big, gruff voice he shouted:

Hold up the prompt card 'You're free!' and encourage the assembly to shout it out.

Show picture 2a. Barabbas was amazed. What about what the crowds had been shouting? Surely they had been shouting 'Kill him! Kill him!'?

The answer was that when the people were shouting 'Kill him!', they were not talking about Barabbas. They were talking about Jesus.

They had been given the choice of having Jesus or Barabbas released, and they chose Barabbas.

But there is a problem. Barabbas was 'guilty' and Jesus wasn't, yet Barabbas was going to be set free and Jesus was going to be killed.

The Bible does not say *why* the people suddenly decided that they wanted Barabbas to be released and Jesus put to death. Maybe Jesus' enemies had told the people untrue stories about Jesus, or maybe they claimed that Barabbas was innocent and shouldn't be in prison.

It does not seem fair, but this means that Jesus took Barabbas' guilt.

And then, when Barabbas was free, Jesus was killed on the cross.

The Bible says that when Jesus died on the cross, he was choosing to take the punishment for all the wrong things all of us have done, not just Barabbas. What an amazing gift! We are probably not murderers, like Barabbas was, but no one is perfect – no one except Jesus.

The Bible says that the punishment for sin is death, and that is why, if Jesus was going to take our punishment, he had to die.

Christians believe that Jesus wants to take the 'guilty' sign away for *all* of the wrong things any of us does or says or even thinks. *Show picture 2b.* Jesus can take away all the wrong things that we do, say and think, but he wasn't guilty of doing anything wrong himself.

Optional prayer time:

Say thank you that Jesus came to earth to take the punishment for all of the wrong things in all of our lives. If you choose to, you could pray that we would think about whether or not we want to accept this gift.

1a

1b

2a

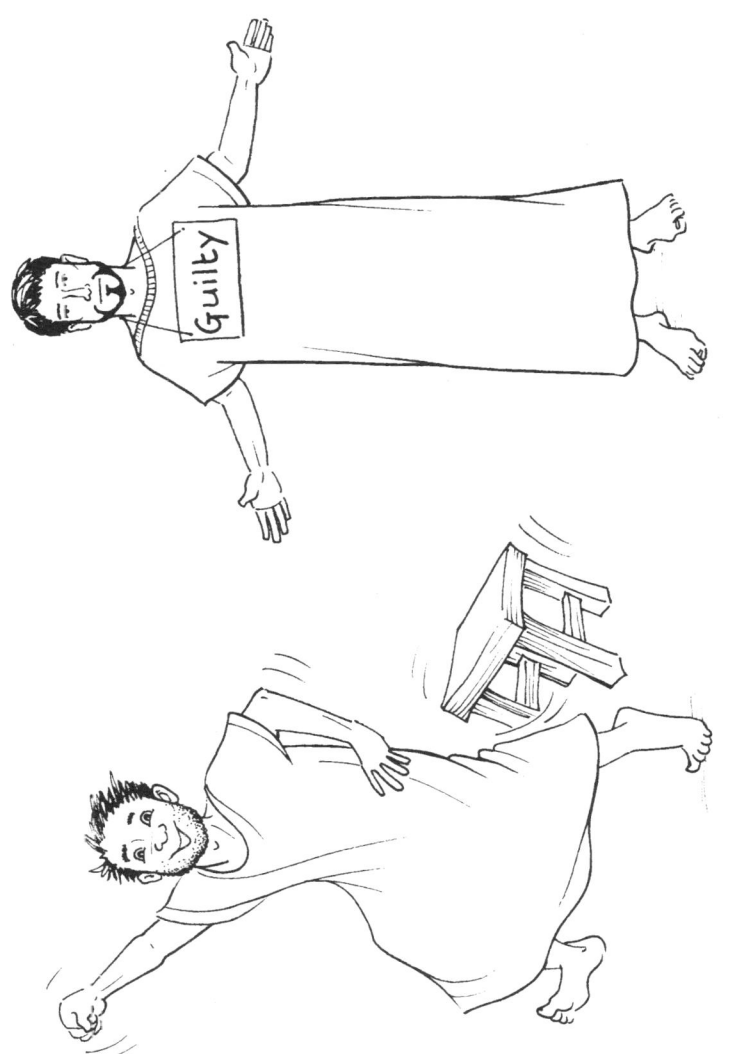

2b

An unbelievable event

2.7

———————— *Bible base: Luke 24:1–12* ————————

Teaching objectives:

To show that the Bible teaches that Jesus came back to life after he was killed.

You will need:
- A large empty matchbox.
- Two sweets.

Introductory activity:

Ask the assembly what makes them think of Easter. Take some suggestions, eg Easter eggs, Easter bunny, daffodils, etc. After you have heard their ideas, show them the large matchbox and say that this reminds you of Easter and you need two volunteers to explain why.

Ask for two volunteers to come to the front. Put a sweet inside the matchbox and give it to your first volunteer, asking them to remove it and eat it. There is no trick!

When they have done this, put another sweet in the box and ask the second person to do the same. However, they will only be allowed to eat the sweet if they manage to get it out of the box and into their mouth without anyone else in the room seeing them, not even you or the other pupil. This means that even if they turn their back, you should still be able to see what they are doing. They are not allowed to leave the room and must stay in front of you!

It's not so easy to remove the sweet without anyone seeing when everyone is watching so closely! *Give the second pupil the sweet*

and ask them both to take their seats again.
Imagine that the matchbox we were just using was a mini model of a tomb, where a body would be laid after a person had died. After Jesus was killed, his body was laid in a tomb which was like a cave, a large stone was rolled in front of the entrance to close the tomb (illustrate this by closing the matchbox) and Roman guards were posted outside to keep watch. There was not much chance of anyone getting the body out of the tomb without the guards noticing and stopping them!
When Jesus' friends came to visit his tomb a couple of days after he was killed, the body was gone (illustrate this by opening the empty matchbox). It would have been impossible for someone to steal it without anyone noticing, and a dead body cannot escape on its own!
When Jesus' followers discovered the tomb was empty, they remembered something he had told them before his crucifixion, which they had not properly understood.
If you are doing this assembly as part of the series 'What's Jesus all about?', refer back to 'A strange twist' and recap on the strange series of events that Jesus told his disciples about. You could re-use the visual aid from that assembly to remind pupils that Jesus had told his disciples this would happen.

Jesus had said that he would be killed and then would be brought back to life again, so it is not that surprising that the tomb was empty. He had already shown that he was someone quite amazing when he had performed miracles. Even though he had died, Jesus came back to life, and some of the people who had known him saw him again before he went to be with God in heaven.

You may have heard of this event. Christians call it the resurrection and it is what is celebrated at Easter.

> **Optional prayer time:**
>
> The resurrection is an unbelievable event; pray that we would expect the unbelievable with God!

An invisible helper

2.8

———————— Bible base: Luke 24:36–53 ————————

Teaching objectives:

To show that Christians believe that, through the Holy Spirit, God is with his people all the time.

> **You will need:**
> - A stereo (not plugged in).
> - A child's windmill.
> - A candle.

Introductory activity:

Choose three volunteers to come to the front. Give each volunteer one of the three objects outlined above. What is it? Can they work out how they would get each thing to work?

Stereo: *plug it in to get power*
Windmill: *blow on it to make it turn*
Candle: *light it to get light and heat*

Each of these things works, but we need to give it some sort of energy first. Can we see the energy that makes the stereo work, or the windmill turn? No, we can only see what the energy makes happen, but that does not mean that we do not believe that electricity and wind exist.

The Bible says that after Jesus rose from the dead, he spent some time with his followers and friends before he went to heaven. His followers did not like the thought that he was going to go away again, and this time for ever!

However, when Jesus went to heaven, he did not leave his

followers on their own. He left them with an invisible helper, someone who would give them energy and help in life. Just like the electricity or wind, this helper would be invisible, but people would be able to see the difference he made. In a way it was like having Jesus with them all the time, but in invisible form.

This invisible helper had an amazing effect on the disciples of Jesus! After Jesus had died, but before he returned to heaven, the disciples had been a bit timid and unsure. After Jesus had gone back to heaven, they were brave and strong and went out to tell everyone about Jesus. With the invisible helper, it was like Jesus was with them all the time, giving them courage.

Can anyone guess who this invisible helper is? The Bible calls him the Holy Spirit and says that through the Holy Spirit, God is always with people who believe in him. The stereo, windmill and candle can help us understand a bit better what the Bible says about him.

Stereo: The stereo needs energy to work. The Bible says that the Holy Spirit is an energy source for God's people. Jesus' followers were really scared after he had been killed, but then, when he sent them the Holy Spirit as their invisible helper, they had courage to go out and tell everyone about Jesus and what he had done.
Windmill: The wind that turns the windmill is invisible. The Bible says that the Holy Spirit is like the wind, because he is invisible, but people can see his effects. When Jesus' followers stood up in front of hundreds of people, everyone could see how brave they were and could hear what they had to say.
Candle: The candle, when it is lit, gives light and heat. Fire always changes things and can be used to get rid of rubbish. The Bible says that the Holy Spirit changes people and gets rid of the bad things in their lives.

The Bible says that Jesus promised that this secret helper – the Holy Spirit – would be given to everyone who chose to be his follower. God would now be living with them every day!

> **Optional prayer time:**
> Pray that we could understand more about what the Bible says about the Holy Spirit, and thank God that he wants to be with us and help us all the time.

The great feast

3.1

―――――― *Bible base: Luke 14:15–24* ――――――

Teaching objectives:

To show that in the Bible Jesus teaches that the kingdom of God is open to anyone who wants to accept the invitation.

You will need:

- Big storybook visual aid (see Introduction on page 6).
- The following list of 'opposites' written on separate sheets of card: Party, Funeral, Feast, Famine, Joy, Sorrow, Dancing, Stillness, Singing, Mourning, Beautiful, Ugly, Peace, War.
- Party invitations (simply squares of card with the words 'You are invited to a party' will do), with the following excuses written on the back:

1. I've just got married. Sorry.
2. I've bought a new car. Sorry, I'm going out for a drive.
3. I've got exams coming up. Sorry, but I've got too much work.
4. I've got a new computer. I want to try it out.
5. I'm getting my hair cut that night. Sorry!
6. I've just met some new friends. Sorry, I'm going out with them.
7. I'm very tired. Sorry, I can't be bothered to come.
8. My favourite band is playing that night. Sorry.
9. There's a big football match on TV that night. Sorry.

- Props for a party (eg shopping bags, small table, a table-cloth, glasses, bottles of lemonade, candles, etc).

Invite two pupils to come to the front. Show the words below to the assembly one by one and ask the volunteers to sort them into opposites, giving all the 'positive' words to one pupil to hold and their opposites to the other.

Party, Funeral, Feast, Famine, Joy, Sorrow, Dancing, Stillness, Singing, Mourning, Beautiful, Ugly, Peace, War.

Review the two sets of words that the pupils are now holding, pointing out that one set is made up of 'positive' words and the other set is made up of their opposites. Explain that today we are going to focus on the positive words because the story Jesus told was about something happy.

Discard the negative list, but keep the pupil there, explaining that you will have a job for them later.

All the words in the positive list are used in the Bible to describe heaven! The Bible describes heaven as being like a party – what an amazing place it must be!

Optional extra activity: play a party game, such as 'Pin the tail on the donkey' or 'Hunt the thimble', to reinforce the message that heaven is described in the Bible as being like a party.

The Bible says that one day, when Jesus was at a party, one of the other guests said that he would love to go to God's party in heaven. So, to explain to the man who would be at God's party, Jesus told him this story:

If you are using it as a visual aid, open the big storybook to make it clear that this is now a made-up story.

One day, a man/woman *(adjust as appropriate to the pupil who had been holding the words)* decided to have a great feast and to invite lots of friends to come and enjoy it with him. So, he went out to deliver the invitations.

Choose nine pupils to come to the front and give them each an invitation which has an excuse written on the back.

Having issued the invitations, all he needed was to get the party prepared. So he called in his servant *(the other pupil who has been holding cards)* and set to work! He bought lots of food and drink, he set the table, he lit candles, and worked and worked until everything was ready.

Use the simple props to set a table for a party.

And so he sent his servant out to let his guests know that everything was ready.

Tell the pupils with invitations to check what the answer is on the back of their invitation. Send the servant to each of the 'guests' in turn to ask them if they want to come or not. The pupils should read out the excuse on their invitation in a loud voice. When all the guests have been asked and have given their response, continue with the story.

None of the guests wanted to come! The man was very angry – he had made so many preparations, and he wanted his house to be full of happy people having fun! So he sent his servant out again to invite all the poor and needy people in the street to come to the party.

Soon the house was full of people who wanted to come to the party.

The feast was the greatest thing these people had ever experienced! They ate and drank and laughed and danced all night!

Close the storybook and ask the pupils at the front to sit down on the floor for the last part of the assembly.

This is the end of the story which the Bible says Jesus told to the man he met at the party. Christians believe that God loves people so much that he wants to throw a big party for them in heaven. In the story, the first people who were invited to the party refused to go because they had other things to do which they thought were more important. The Bible says that people accept God's invitation to heaven by making him the most important person in their life.

> **Optional prayer time:**
>
> Use the positive words listed at the beginning to think about the Bible's description of heaven.

The story of the lost son

3.2

Bible base: Luke 15:11–32

Teaching objectives:

To show that Christians believe that God's forgiveness is available to anyone who is truly sorry for the wrong things they have done.

> **You will need:**
>
> - Big storybook visual aid.
> - The following words written in sections on separate large pieces of paper or on acetate: IN TRO DUCT ION; CIR CUM STA NCES; UND ERST AND ING; MUL TIPLI CAT ION; SOR RY.
> - A newspaper.
> - A card with the following words written on it for a pupil to read out: 'I was wrong to leave you and spend all my money. I don't deserve to be your son any more. Can I be your servant?'
>
> *Optional:*
>
> - Simple costumes for characters (two sons and father, eg a baseball cap for younger son, a woolly hat for older son and a flat cap for father).

The story in this outline is an improvised drama of the Bible story involving pupils acting out the parts. It is essential that you are very familiar with the story in advance to enable you to relax and help the pupils in their improvisation. It is great fun, however, and pupils generally enjoy it and perform well!

Introductory activity:

Show the assembly each of the difficult words in a mixed-up order. Can anyone work out what the word is? (If the school you are in has a long name, you could add it to the list.)

    IN TRO DUCT ION
    CIR CUM STA NCES
    UND ERST AND ING
    MUL TIPLI CAT ION
    SOR RY

The last word was much easier, but actually, while 'sorry' is not a hard word to say, it is very hard to really mean it.

Jesus told a story about saying sorry and what happens when we say sorry to God. *Open the storybook visual aid if you are using it for this section.*

    Once upon a time there was a man. *(Choose a pupil to be the father and give him his costume.)* This man had a farm (*ask pupils to make animal noises*) and on that farm he also had two sons *(choose two other pupils, preferably one older and one younger pupil and give them costumes).*

    Now, the father loved his sons very much *(if they will, get the 'father' to put his arm round his 'sons'' shoulders)* and enjoyed having them around the farm with him. The father had worked very hard to build up his farm *(mime digging)*. The older son was a hard worker too *(digging)* and worked out in the fields from when he woke up in the morning until he went to bed at night. The younger son, however, preferred to stay inside. In fact, not only did he prefer to stay inside, he preferred to stay in bed all day. When he woke up *(mime waking up)*, he liked to go straight back to sleep *(snore)*. Meanwhile, his brother and his dad did all the work *(digging)*.

    One day, however, as he lay in bed, avoiding all work, he had an idea *(ask the pupil to pretend to have an idea by looking suddenly very alert)*. His father, he knew, was a very wealthy man, as he had worked so hard all his life *(check that the older son and father are still digging)*. When he died, his two sons would get all his money. So, why didn't he go to his father now and ask him for the money? There was no point waiting until his father died – he might be too old to enjoy it by then!

    So, off he went to find his dad – who was digging – to ask him for his share of the money. *The younger son should go to his dad, put out his hands and ask for his money.* What do you think his father said? *Ask the pupils what they think.*

Perhaps it's hard to believe, but his father said yes! He gave him the money and so, the next day, the younger son packed his bags and set off on an adventure! He had never had so much money in his life! He was very excited! *Ask the pupil to look very excited.*

Eventually he came to a country far from home where the weather was good and the people were friendly and life was cheap, so he settled down to some serious spending! *Ask the pupil to mime throwing money around.*

As you can imagine, the man found it very easy to find friends when he was throwing his money around. *Choose some more pupils to come to the front as his friends.* All they had to do was put out their hands *(mime)* and he would give them as much money as they wanted. He was very popular!

Meanwhile, back at home, while his older brother worked in the fields *(mime digging)* his father would sometimes stop and think about his younger son. He would look out along the road, hoping to see him coming home *(ask the pupil to mime shielding his eyes to look out into the distance).*

One day, when the younger son was out with all his new friends, not thinking about his old dad at all, he suddenly realised that he had no money left – his pockets were completely empty *(mime).* And now that he had no money left, his new friends were not so interested in him any more and off they went to find someone else to be their friend. *Ask the other pupils to sit at the side for the rest of the story.* They had only liked him because he gave them money. The younger son was very sad *(mime).*

For the first time in his life he was going to have to do some work! So, he looked in the paper to see what job he could do *(give the pupil a newspaper).* He didn't want to do anything too hard or messy, but the only thing that he could find, after much searching, was the most disgusting job he could think of: feeding pigs.

Yuck! It was such a smelly job that he had to hold his nose with one hand while feeding the pigs with the other *(mime).* He got paid almost nothing and gradually the younger son got weaker and weaker, and more and more hungry, until he sat down and cried *(mime).*

What was he doing? He started to think of home where, as we all know, his brother and his father were working *(mime digging)* and felt very sad. Why had he run away and wasted all his money? Even his dad's servants had a better life than he had now.

But he was scared to go home. What would his dad say? Would he be cross? He didn't deserve to be taken back by his father.

But then, he had an idea *(mime having an idea again)*. What if he went back and asked his dad to take him on as a servant? Then he would be back at home, near his dad and his brother, and he wouldn't be as hungry and miserable as he was now.

So, he picked himself up *(mime)*, dusted himself down *(mime)* and set off on the long journey home *(mime)*.

Meanwhile, back at home, can you guess what was happening? His brother was digging *(mime)* and his dad was doing some digging *(mime)* while also looking out along the road *(mime)*, in the hope that his younger son might eventually come back.

The younger son walked and walked and walked *(mime)* until he thought he could walk no more! Just as he was getting too tired and hungry and weak to go on, he suddenly spotted something on the horizon. It was his home! He was so excited that, even though he was so tired, he jumped for joy *(mime)*! He was nervous about seeing his dad, but he had his lines ready. He'd been practising it the whole way home! *Give the pupil the card to read out.* When he saw his dad he would say:

(Pupil reads) 'I was wrong to leave you and spend all my money. I don't deserve to be your son any more. Can I be your servant?'

Back at the farm, his dad too had caught sight of something exciting. *Father should be shielding his eyes and looking into the distance.* As he looked down the road, he thought he saw his son in the distance! And as the person got closer, he knew for sure that it was his son! He too jumped for joy *(mime)* and ran out to meet his son *(mime)*.

When they met, his father gave him a huge hug! *(It is unlikely that the pupils will act this out!)* The son told his father what he had been practising all the way home:

Pupil should repeat the words on the card:

'I was wrong to leave you and spend all my money. I don't deserve to be your son any more. Can I be your servant?'

But his father loved him so much that he was delighted to have him back as his son! He ordered his servants to prepare a huge party and get the best clothes for his younger son and invited everyone to come and join the celebration. *The father and younger son should start pretending to dance!*

The older son, meanwhile, was still out in the fields, digging *(mime)*, and when he heard the party, he was very cross. He had worked for his father for years and yet when his little brother came home, having wasted everything, he got a party! He was raging (mime)!

But his father went out to him and asked him to come in and join the party. *Father should go over to the older son and invite him to the party.*

The man had two sons, and he loved them both. One of them had always been there, and everything the father had was his, but he had to celebrate when the son he had lost came home again! *Thank the pupils for their help and ask them to take their seats again.*

The younger son knew that he had been stupid and had given up all that he had at home to go off and do his own thing. He had to be ready to go back and say sorry. But the father loved him so much that he was just pleased to have him back. He didn't want to punish him – he wanted to celebrate!

In the Bible Jesus said that this story was a picture of what God thinks about us. He said that God is like the father and loves us so much that he wants to forgive us when we come to him to say sorry for the things we do that are wrong.

As we said at the beginning, sorry is a very hard thing to say, both to God and to other people. But Christians believe that we don't need to be scared of saying sorry to God because he loves us and will forgive us.

Optional prayer time:

Thank God that he will forgive us when we say sorry to him.

The Pharisee and the tax collector

3.3

———— *Bible base: Luke 18:9–14* ————

Teaching objectives:

To teach that Christians believe God will listen to anyone who wants to talk to him.

> **You will need:**
> - Big storybook visual aid.
> - Pictures on page 74 photocopied on to acetate or card.
>
> *Optional:*
> - Prayers below on acetate.

Introductory activity:

Read out, or display on acetate, the following 'prayers', asking pupils to tell you which ones they think are 'real' prayers and which ones are not.

'God, I don't know why I'm feeling the way I do. I just feel lonely and confused. It seems like no one understands me. I hope you understand me.'

'Lord God, thou who made the heavens and the earth and all that therein lies, bless your people on this thy day.'

'It's not fair! I thought you were supposed to love me, God, but it just seems like everything's going wrong and you don't hear me… WHY?'

'Help! Is there anyone there?'

'Our Father, who art in heaven, hallowed be thy name…'

'God, I don't really think I believe in you at all!'

All of these might be prayers. Prayer is about communicating honestly with God, not about simply saying a set of words that we've learnt as a 'prayer'. So, if I say the Lord's Prayer from memory while thinking about what I'm going to watch on TV later, I'm not praying. But if I really speak to God honestly, that is praying.

Jesus told a story to help us understand what prayer is and who can pray.

Open storybook if using it as a visual aid.

The story was about two very different men. One of them was a very religious person. How would a very religious person feel and act in church? *(eg he would know what to do, he would feel very confident, he would pray, etc.)* How would he stand?

Show the picture of the Pharisee (on the left) from page 74.

This is what the religious person said when he 'prayed':

'I thank you, God, *(pause)* that I am not a bad person like everyone else, *(pause)* especially like that tax collector over there! *(pause)* For I never cheat, *(pause)* I don't do bad things, *(pause)* I don't lie, *(pause)* I fast twice a week, *(pause)* and I give you a tenth of my money.'

The other man in the story was a thief. How would he feel in church? *(eg ashamed, embarrassed, inferior to all the 'religious' people.)*

Show the picture of the tax collector (on the right) from page 74.

The Bible says that the thief stood away at a distance and would not even lift his eyes from looking at the floor. It even says he beat his chest in sorrow as he said these words:

'O God *(pause)*, forgive me *(pause)*, for I have done lots of bad things.'

Which prayer do you think God hears? Remember that prayer is communicating honestly with God. Do you think the religious person was honest? Even good people have done something wrong!

Close the storybook if you were using it.

Christians believe that Jesus told this story to show people that God listens to anyone who really wants to talk to him honestly. Christians believe that we can tell God when we are cross or confused, happy or excited, and if we are honest with him, then he can do something about it.

Optional prayer time:

Give thanks that God will always listen to us and that there is nothing we cannot say to him. Ask God to help us to be more honest with him.

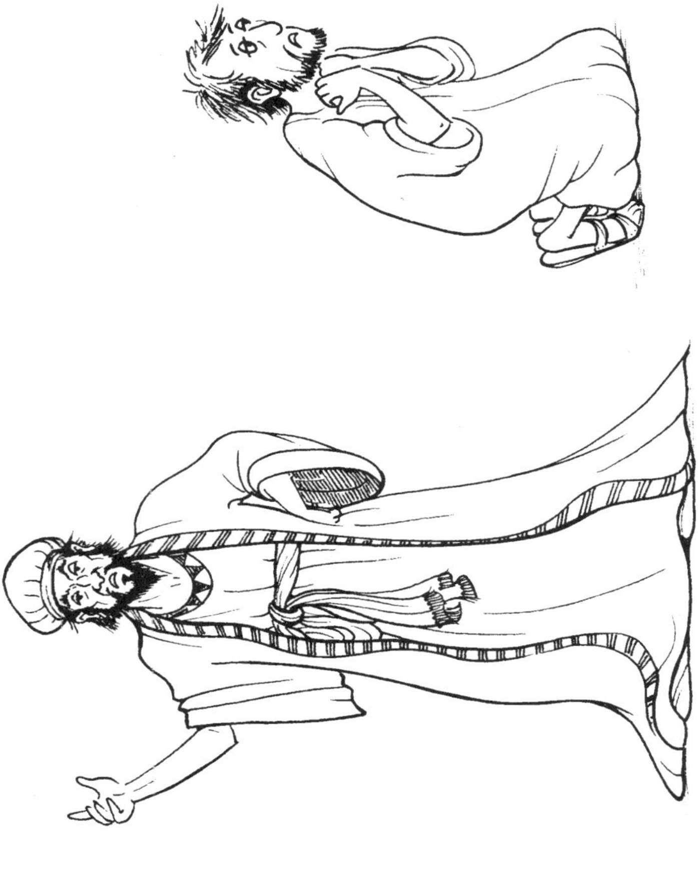

The story of the sower

3.4

――― *Bible base: Luke 8:4–15* ―――

Teaching objectives:

To show that the message of the Bible is there for anyone who wants to take notice of it.

You will need:
- A Bible.
- Big storybook visual aid.
- A bag of seeds (perhaps a well secured cloth bag filled with beans).
- A brick.
- A piece of green carpet or a green camping mat.
- Some rope.
- A green cushion.
- Some magazines.

Introductory activity:

Call out the following words, and ask the pupils to put their hand up if they know what the words mean:

'Timber!'	(falling tree)
'SOS!'	(help)
'Fore!'	(golf ball on its way)
'On your marks, get set…'	(get ready to start a race)
'Blast off!'	(something is being launched)

Make the point that there is a difference between hearing and understanding these words. If we don't understand them, we won't act on them. Yet sometimes it is important to act on them or else there could be a nasty accident!

Jesus knew the difference between hearing and understanding. He told a story and asked people to listen to it first and then he would help them to understand what it meant. So the first part of this assembly is the listening bit!

Choose four volunteers to help you re-tell the story of the farmer sowing the seed. Tell the story as follows, opening up the 'storybook' if using it as a visual aid:

Once upon a time, there was a farmer who went out to sow seed on his land.

Throw the bag of seeds for the first volunteer to catch.

This person *(use their name)* has just become some seed! Some seed fell on the path.

Give volunteer 1 a brick and ask them to sit on it. Ask them how comfortable it is. Ask them how long they would like to sit there.

A path was not a very good place for a seed to land. It was hard and stony and lumpy and altogether very unpleasant. And what was worse, there were lots of people who would walk on your head *(reassure the pupil that you won't act that bit out!)* and then, if you hadn't been completely squashed to bits, you would end up being eaten up by the birds.

Volunteer 1 should keel over and 'die'. Ask the child to remain at the front of the assembly until all four 'seeds' have finished (otherwise it will be distracting.)

Not a very long and happy life for the seed that landed on the path!

Retrieve the bag of seeds and throw it to the second volunteer. Tell them that it is their turn to 'be' the seed.

Some seed fell on shallow ground, which looked nice and green and pleasant, but the soil was not very deep.

Give volunteer 2 a piece of green carpet (or a camping mat) with a brick underneath it to sit on. Ask them if it is comfortable. Ask them how long they would like to sit there.

This seed was much better off than the seed that landed on the path. At first, it was comfortable enough, but the longer it lay there, the less comfortable it became. Seeds need lots of goodness from the earth to grow, and there really wasn't enough soil on this ground for the seed to grow properly. So, soon after it began to grow (*get the pupil to start to get up on to their feet*) it ran out of food and water and fell over and died.

Pupil should respond accordingly, but then remain at the front of the room with volunteer 1. Retrieve the bag of seeds and throw it to the third volunteer, telling them it is their turn to be the seed.

Still more seed fell amongst thorns.

Give volunteer 3 the piece of green carpet or a camping mat to sit on with ropes lying on top of it. Ask them how comfortable they feel. Ask them how long they would like to sit there.

This ground had deep soil, with no rocks just under the surface, and so the seed began to grow. It grew and grew and grew (*volunteer 3 should gradually stand up*) and soon became a tall, slender plant. But there were also weeds on this ground, and no sooner had the plant grown up, than the weeds began to choke the young plant.

Begin to wrap the ropes around them as you tell the story, but be very careful not to alarm or hurt the child with the rope.

And so, gradually, the weeds became too big and too strong for the poor plant to survive, and it was choked to death by the weeds.

Pupil should pretend to die. Be careful they don't do this too extravagantly and get rope burns. The pupil should remain at the front of the room with the others. Retrieve the bag of seeds and throw it to the fourth volunteer who is now the seed.

Finally, some seed fell on good soil.

Give volunteer 4 the carpet or camping mat with a cushion on it to sit on. Ask them how comfortable it is.

Now this ground was perfect for the seed to grow. The soil was deep and full of goodness. The seed grew up to be a strong plant (*pupil should stand up*). And then, as a strong, healthy plant, that little seed produced lots more seeds, so more plants could grow. *Bring the other pupils over to join the 'good seed' on the 'good soil'.*

Close the storybook, if you have been using it, and make it clear to the assembly that this is the end of the story that Jesus told.

We have all heard the story, but have we understood it? Just like the words we looked at earlier, it is important to both hear and understand the story. Thankfully, in the Bible, Jesus actually explained what the story meant!

Explain the story as follows:

(In a multi-faith setting, ask the pupils to take their seats before you begin to explain the meaning, and illustrate the different reactions to God and the Bible yourself rather than asking pupils to open or pretend to read the Bible.)

What happened to the first volunteer's seeds? *They were eaten up.*

The Bible says that this is the reaction of some people to God. When they think about the Bible, they don't want to really listen and understand and so they don't even open it up. *Hand the Bible to the first pupil closed, then take it away again.*

What happened to the second volunteer's seeds? *They died very quickly.*

This is what happens to some people when they hear the Bible. They listen at first and believe what they hear, but after a while they lose interest. *Hand the open Bible to the second pupil, but then take it away again almost immediately.*

What happened to the third volunteer's seeds? *They were choked by the weeds.*

This is what happens to some other people when they hear God's word in the Bible. They are really interested at first, but then other things distract them. *Give the third pupil the open Bible, but then as they are looking at it, set some magazines on top of it.*

What happened to the fourth volunteer's seeds? *They grew into a strong plant.*

This is what happens when people want to hear God's Word. If they really listen, Jesus says they will hear and understand. *Hand the open Bible to the fourth pupil who should pretend to read it.*

Optional prayer time:

Sum up the assembly by explaining that Christians believe that the Bible is God's Word and he will help us to understand it if we really want to hear what he's got to say. Pray that God will help them to understand the Bible.

Power over circumstances

4.1

―――――― *Bible base: Luke 9:10–17* ――――――

Teaching objectives:

To show that Christians believe Jesus has power in situations that seem to have no solution.

> **You will need:**
>
> - A Smarties tube with the plastic seal intact, but emptied from the bottom.
> - A soft drinks can, again emptied from a hole in the bottom.
> - A lunch box with five small rolls and two small tins of sardines.
> - Flip chart and pen – or find out if the school chef is happy to speak in the assembly.

Introductory activity:

Choose two volunteers and ask them, without touching either object, to inspect both the Smarties tube and the can.

Do they both look 'normal'?

Give one to each pupil. What is wrong with it? Why were they surprised? Did they think it would be full?

This was a trick. It looked as though I was being really generous and was giving them a full tube of Smarties and a can of drink, but they were actually empty. The volunteers know that it was a trick because they haven't tasted the contents!

Today's story is about an event from the Bible which could have looked like a magic trick with food, but Christians believe it was not. The people involved knew they had been well fed.

This is what the Bible says happened: Jesus was teaching lots of people who had travelled from miles around to hear what he had to say. By the end of the day there were about five thousand people all gathered on a hillside, listening to Jesus' teaching. But the people had been listening to Jesus for a long time and hadn't brought any food with them, and so, as it was getting late, they were beginning to get hungry. The disciples were worried about the people being hungry, so eventually they went to Jesus and asked him to send the people away to find food and lodging for the night.

Jesus' response was a bit of a surprise! He told the disciples to feed the crowd! Who can remember how many people there were? Where would they ever find enough food to feed them?

The disciples went to tell the people to find what food they could, but between them, all they could find was one person's lunch (*open lunch box*) – five small rolls and two fish. How far would that go? Either two people would be quite well filled, or about ten people would get a bite to eat.

At this point, if you have a friendly chef in the school you could interview them quickly about how many pupils are in the school, how much food it takes to feed all the pupils and how long it takes to get it ready. Alternatively, you could choose a volunteer to tell you what is in their lunch box and multiply it by 5,000, writing the results on a flip chart at the front.

To us, five small rolls and two fish would not be much help in this situation, but with Jesus, nothing was impossible. Once the disciples gave the lunch to Jesus, he took it and gave thanks to God for what little they had. Then he instructed the disciples to start giving it out to all the people.

Start to give out the rolls and sardines.

Unlike my lunch here, the rolls and fish just kept on coming until everyone had had enough to eat. Not only that, but when the disciples gathered up the leftovers, there were 12 full baskets!

How does the Bible say the people could be sure that it was not a trick? Because they were full! They had each been given more than enough to eat, because Jesus had the power to change a little bit of food into a lot. Christians believe that even in circumstances where there doesn't seem to be any solution, Jesus has power to change things if we will trust him with what we have.

Optional prayer time:

Think of some of the difficult situations in the world at this time and ask God to show his power in them. Thank him that he has power over these situations and also the smaller situations in our own lives.

Power over life and death

4.2

Bible base: Luke 8:40–56

Teaching objectives:

To show that Christians believe Jesus has power over life and death.

> **You will need:**
> - Three pieces of newspaper (one double broadsheet page, one single broadsheet page and half a single broadsheet page).
> - Four faces from the template on page 86 photocopied on to acetate or card.

Introductory activity:

Bring three pupils to the front and give each of them one of the pieces of newspaper. Ask them how many times they think they could double over their piece of paper. Do they think the person with the biggest piece of paper could fold it more times? Ask them to try it out. Can they reach their total? Regardless of the size, they should not be able to fold it any more than seven times.

It is hard to believe, but no matter how big the bit of paper is, it is impossible to fold it more than seven times. In today's story, the Bible says Jesus does something that seems impossible for two different people.

Tell the following story as dramatically as possible.

There were four people in this story who were very unhappy. The first of these four people was a man (*display one of the faces at the front of the assembly looking unhappy*). He was unhappy because his 12-year-old daughter was very ill and if she didn't get help, she would die. That meant that not only the man, but also his wife and his little girl, were very unhappy *(display another two faces at the front of the assembly looking unhappy)*.

The man's name was Jairus and he knew that Jesus had healed lots of people who weren't well. So he asked him to come to see his little girl.

But there was still one more unhappy person. This person was a woman who had been ill for 12 years – the whole of the little girl's lifetime. She had spent all the money that she had on doctors, but none of them had been able to help her *(display the last face at the front of the assembly looking unhappy)*.

This woman was in the crowd when Jairus came to ask for Jesus' help. She wanted so much to get near enough to Jesus to be able to ask him to heal her.

But suddenly she realised that Jesus was walking away! Jairus had spoken to him and he was going to help the little girl. The woman desperately wanted Jesus to help her. What could she do? She was so weak.

But, with one last effort, she pushed and shoved her way through the people in front of her until she got near enough to just be able to stretch out her fingertips to touch his robe. That might be enough to make her well!

As soon as she touched him, she knew that something amazing had happened. She knew that her illness had been cured. Instantly, the woman who had been so sad for 12 years was happy! Her life had been turned around! *Turn her unhappy face around so that it is a happy face.*

She wasn't the only one who noticed that something had happened. Jesus had noticed too, because he felt power go out from him. As soon as she had touched his robe, he stopped to find out who had touched him. Even though the crowds were pressing in on him on all sides, he knew that someone had touched him believing that he could heal them. Jesus asked who it was, and the woman spoke to him.

The woman was now happy because, as she had hoped, Jesus had made her well again.

But there are still three unhappy people in the story – Jairus, his wife and his little girl *(indicate the unhappy faces at the front)*. In fact, the story was about to become even sadder, because as Jesus spoke to the woman, a servant came from Jairus' house to say that the little girl had died *(remove the girl's face)*. So now that the little girl was dead, Jairus and his wife were even more unhappy. If only Jesus hadn't stopped to talk to the woman, maybe the little girl would not have died.

But Jesus simply told Jairus to believe and not to worry. So even though the girl was dead, Jesus carried on to Jairus' house.

When he got there, all the people were weeping and wailing and mourning for the little girl. They didn't think there was anything anyone could do to help.

But Jesus seemed to think there was something he could do. Jesus went in, took the little girl by the hand and told her to get up – and she did!

So now, instead of three very unhappy people and one dead person, there were four people who were happier than they had ever been and had experienced some really exciting and life-changing things! *Replace the fourth face and turn it and the other two sad faces around so that they are happy.* The woman had suffered for 12 years, and now her life had been turned around so that she could live a healthy and normal life. Jairus and his wife had their lives turned around when their little girl was healed. And the little girl really did get her life turned around – in fact, she came back to life! Jesus healed the woman and the little girl because people believed in his power.

Christians believe that Jesus has power over life and death. He was able to give people back happiness in life when they were miserable, and he was even able to give people back life itself!

> **Optional prayer time:**
>
> Say thank you that Jesus has power to help people when their life is really hard. When people believe in his power, he can do amazing things and turn people's lives around.

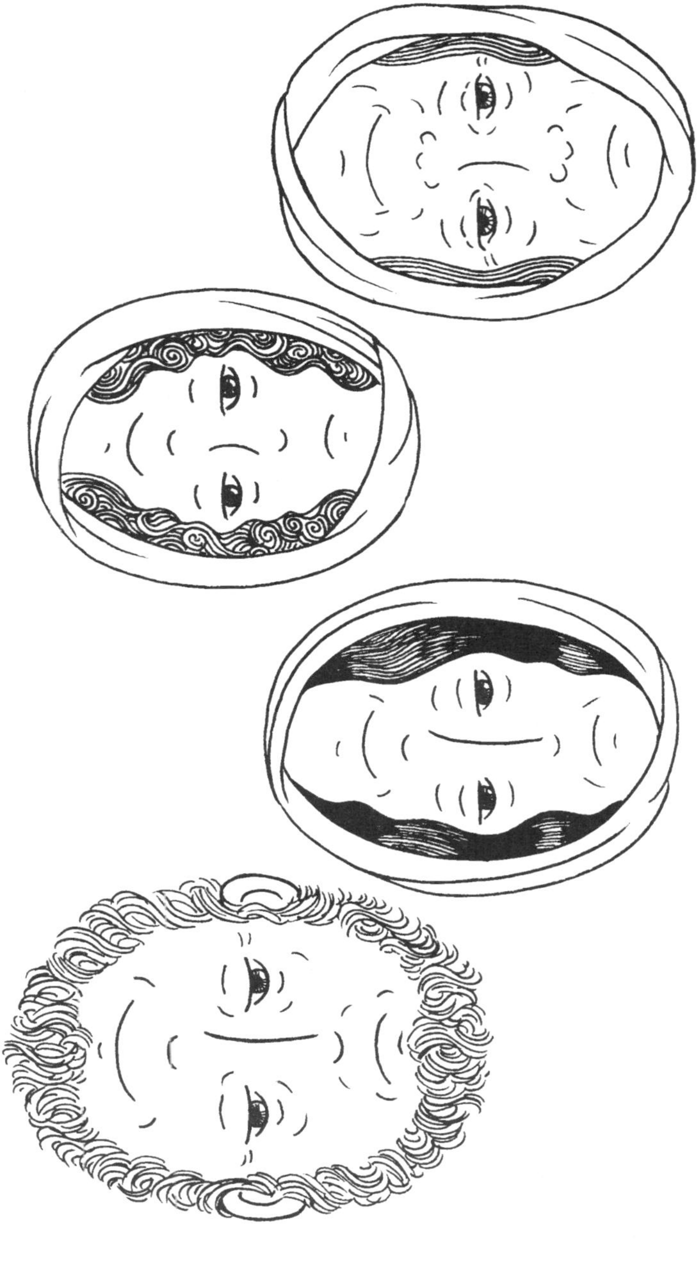

Power over nature

4.3

―――――― *Bible base: Luke 8:22–25* ――――――

Teaching objectives:

To show that the Bible says Jesus had power to control nature.

> **You will need:**
> - Ten A4 pieces of paper each with a letter of the word IMPOSSIBLE written on it.

Introductory activity:

Nature quiz. Show the pupils each letter in turn and give them the corresponding clue. The letters make up the word 'IMPOSSIBLE'. When a pupil gives you the right answer, call them to the front to hold up the appropriate letter.

P   A black and white bird which cannot fly and lives at the South Pole (*penguin*)
I   A large floating piece of frozen water near the North or South Pole (*iceberg*)
M It shines brightly at night (*moon*)
O Round juicy fruit with a thick brightly coloured skin (*orange*)
S   Ball of fire in the sky that gives us light (*sun*)
L   A big cat with a furry mane (*lion*)
S   Creature that spins a web (*spider*)
I   Small six-legged creature (*insect*)
E   Another name for the world (*earth*)
B   Feathered creature (*bird*)

What do the letters spell? Unscramble them to find out. (IMPOSSIBLE)

Take the letters from the pupils and display them at the front to be referred to later. Ask the pupils to take their seats again.

Each of these things is amazing – it would be impossible for us to make any of them ourselves. We can alter our world or damage it through pollution and misuse, but we can never really control it.
Tell the story of Jesus calming the storm from Luke 8:22–25, as outlined below. Encourage pupil participation when they hear the following prompts, asking them to stop when you give them the signal:

asleep snore
boat sway from side to side
afraid scream
wind blow
storm divide assembly into four groups to make the following sounds: 'whoosh!', 'swish', tapping floor with fingers, clapping

The Bible says that one day, after Jesus had been talking to large crowds of people, he suggested to the disciples that they take a **boat** out and cross over to the other side of the lake. Now, the disciples thought this was a great idea. The people had been around for ages and the disciples were really quite tired and glad of an excuse to get away for a bit. So, they all got into the **boat** and set off across the lake. The further out from shore they got, the more the **boat** swayed, and before they knew it, Jesus had fallen sound **asleep**.

Soon the disciples too began to get a bit drowsy. But before they could fall **asleep**, they noticed a small cloud in the distance. Soon the small cloud became a huge black cloud and the **wind** began to blow. The **wind** got stronger and stronger, the waves grew higher and higher and the disciples grew more and more **afraid**. Suddenly, they were in the middle of a huge **storm** and they were all **afraid** for their lives!

All, that is, except Jesus. Throughout it all, as the **wind** blew and the **boat** lurched from side to side and the **storm** raged, Jesus was still **asleep**! What were they to do? Jesus was supposed to be their leader – he had done so many amazing things – and now they were all going to drown while he slept!

Quickly, they woke him up shouting, 'Master, Master, we're going to drown!' *You may wish to get the assembly to shout these words out.*

When Jesus looked at the sea and saw the huge **storm** that had blown up, he told it to stop – and it did! *Signal for them to stop abruptly.*

'Where is your faith?' Jesus asked them. Jesus wanted his disciples to trust him. And when the disciples saw that the **wind** had died down, they were amazed and asked themselves who exactly this man could be, that even nature obeyed him!

All the things we talked about at the beginning of the assembly are amazing parts of the natural world that it would be impossible for us to control. Yet the Bible says that Jesus had power even over nature!

> **Optional prayer time:**
>
> Lead the pupils in the following prayer, encouraging them to keep looking to the front and shouting out 'impossible!' when you point to it.
>
> Lord Jesus, thank you that nothing is impossible for you. Thank you that you have power over nature, that you have power over illness, that you have power over everything! When we think that something is impossible, help us to come to you and ask you for help. With your help, nothing is impossible!
>
> *As an alternative to praying, say the following statement about Christian belief, encouraging the pupils to shout out 'IMPOSSIBLE' with you:*
>
> Christians believe that nothing is IMPOSSIBLE for God. They believe that he has power over nature, power over illness, power over everything! Sometimes we come across things in life that we think are IMPOSSIBLE – Christians believe that God can help us, even with these IMPOSSIBLE things.

Power over sin

4.4

──────── *Bible base: Luke 5:17–26* ────────

Teaching objectives:

To show that the Bible says Jesus had exceptional power to forgive the things that we do wrong. This backed up his claim to be the Son of God.

> **You will need:**
> - A stereo that does not work (if that is hard to find, detach the wiring in the plug, but leave the plug attached to the flex).
> - A jacket with the words 'I can't walk' attached with safety pins to the outside and 'I have done things that are wrong', 'I have bad attitudes' and 'I am not perfect' safety-pinned to the inside.

Introductory activity:

Show the stereo to the pupils and tell them that you are going to play some great music to them (you could get quite excited about this!). Make sure that the stereo is not plugged in and that this is visible to the assembly. Also, make sure that there is no CD in the player. Make a big show of pressing 'play' and then pretend to be confused because nothing happens. Can they spot what is wrong?

Once they have spotted that it is not plugged in and you have fixed this, press 'play' again and wait for the music. Can anyone guess what's wrong this time? Open the CD player to check that the CD is in correctly, but of course, the CD is not there.

Put a CD in the player and again build up to pressing 'play' and waiting for the music. What is wrong this time? The CD player is plugged in, the CD is in, but it still will not play.

The CD player is broken inside. Although it looks fine on the outside, and although all the obvious problems are now fixed, there is still a bigger problem inside.

Today's story from the Bible is about a man who had two problems, one obvious and one hidden inside.

Choose a volunteer to come to the front and dress them in the jacket with the words 'I can't walk' visible to the assembly. Ask them to sit on a seat at the front.

Everyone who walked past this man as he sat in the street knew what the problem was, because it was obvious. Everyone could see that he couldn't walk. This problem was on the outside.

But, just like the stereo, this man also had a problem inside, although he may not have realised exactly what this problem was. Actually, this is a problem that we all have.

Although this man could not walk and run about with his friends, he did have some very special friends who cared for him and spent time with him. These friends wanted to do anything they could to help their friend to walk again. They knew that Jesus had helped lots of people, and so they took their friend to him.

They had to try really hard to get to Jesus. He was so popular that the house where he was staying was packed with people. They actually had to go up on the roof and lower their friend down on his mat to Jesus. I wonder what they thought Jesus would say? He had healed lots of people simply by saying something. Would he just say 'Get up', or would he touch the man's feet and say 'Be healed'?

Jesus actually said a very strange thing! He said:

'My friend, your sins are forgiven.'

Sin means anything we have done or said or thought that makes us less then perfect. *Ask the members of staff in the assembly if anyone in the room is perfect.* No one is perfect. We have all done some of the wrong things the Bible calls 'sin'.

So, when Jesus said that the man's sins were forgiven, he meant that all the things he had done or said or thought in the past that were less than perfect were forgotten about by God!

Some people were very cross! Who did Jesus think he was? How could he say that he forgave the man for everything he had ever done wrong? They believed only God could do that.

The answer is in the hidden problem that this man had inside. Just like the stereo which was not plugged in, there was something very obvious wrong with the man – he could not walk. But what was wrong inside was more serious. *Ask the volunteer to open the jacket to reveal the words written inside –* 'I have done things that are wrong', 'I have bad attitudes', 'I am not perfect'.

These were the problems that Jesus was dealing with first, because they were more serious than the problem which everyone else could see.

Once Jesus had forgiven the man, he *did* tell the man to pick up his mat and walk home. And that is exactly what the man did! The man went home healed, not just on the outside, but on the inside too.

As you are saying this, take the jacket from the pupil and ask them to return to their seat. Put the jacket on yourself. Take the sign from the outside.

As a Christian, I believe that the problems that I have on the outside may be different to those of the man in the story, but the problem on the inside is the same for everyone. Christians believe that Jesus can deal with all the other problems in our life too, but the main thing he wants to deal with first is the problem on the inside. What is that problem? It's the fact that we aren't perfect and have done and said things that are wrong – what the Bible calls 'sin'. Christians believe that God wants to forgive us, just as Jesus forgave the man in today's story.

> **Optional prayer time:**
>
> Give thanks that God wants to deal with the wrong things in our life and to forgive us.

Power to teach

4.5

--- *Bible base: Luke 11:1–13* ---

Teaching objectives:

To show that the Bible says Jesus had power to talk to God and to teach others how to talk to him.

You will need:

- Three or four scarves (or lengths of rope).
- A copy of the visual aid from page 98, either copied on to flip chart paper, or photocopied on to acetate. The solution is given and you may want to practise beforehand!
- Red, green and orange paints or marker pens, or OHP pens.

Introductory activity:

Show the pupils one of the scarves, tied in a knot. Ask for two or three volunteers to come to the front and tie another scarf/rope in a knot like the one you have just shown them.

After the volunteers have tied the scarves in a knot, explain that you managed to tie yours without lifting your hands off either end of the scarf. Each of them had to lift one hand off the scarf to tie it. Ask them if they think they could do it without taking their hands off.

Allow them to try for a few minutes, tying themselves in knots while you assure them that it is possible! (By picking the scarf up by either end with arms unfolded it will always be impossible to tie it in a knot without releasing one end.)

When they have given up, untie your scarf and show them how you did it. You should fold your arms in the conventional way, placing one hand over and one hand under the other arm. From this position, pick up one end of the scarf in each hand and simply unfold your arms. A knot will be tied in the scarf.

Allow them to try using this new method.

Ask the children to take their seats again. Although I told you it was possible, you didn't know how to do it until I showed you the right way. Once I taught you, then you were able to do it for yourself.

Have you ever watched someone doing something and wondered if you could do it too? Maybe you've watched a magician performing a trick, or watched your favourite footballer do a really clever move, and you've wanted to learn how to do it.

In today's story, Jesus' disciples watched him praying. When the Bible talks about praying, it means talking to God. The disciples wanted to know how to talk to God the way Jesus did!

So, when Jesus had finished praying, the disciples asked him if he would teach them how to talk to God. What he taught them is written on this sheet of paper/on the screen.

Show the pupils the visual aid you have prepared.

It's not very clear, is it? Perhaps this is how the disciples felt about prayer. They had watched Jesus talking to God but they weren't sure how they could do it themselves.

Let's see if we can discover three things that Jesus told them about prayer.

Start to paint or colour the first word on the sheet in red: LOVE

The first thing he told them was that they should love God. The Bible says that he told them to pray:

'Our Father in heaven, hallowed be your name.'

This means that God should be really special to them. He should be more important than anyone else. Jesus was telling them that they should tell God how great he is and how much they love him!

Paint or colour the second word on the sheet in orange: ASK

The second thing he told them was that they should ask God for whatever they needed. The Bible says he told them to say:

'Give us this day our daily bread.'

This doesn't just mean that they should ask him for bread! Jesus wanted them to ask God for everything that they needed for life. They could go to him for anything and he would hear them.

Paint or colour the third word on the sheet in green: SORRY

The third thing they were to say to God was sorry. Jesus told them to say:

'Forgive us our sins.'

When the Bible uses the word 'sin', it means anything we do or say or think that is wrong. The Bible says that these things hurt God. So Jesus told his disciples to say sorry to God for all the wrong things they had done that God didn't like.

So, these three words sum up the first bit of what Jesus told his disciples about prayer. They should love God first and praise him for how great he is. They should ask him for whatever they needed. And they should say sorry to him for the wrong things they had done.

But then Jesus went on to explain something else about prayer. Perhaps the colours we have used to paint these words will help us to discover what else he told them. Do these colours remind you of anything?

Red, amber and green are the colours of traffic lights. What does each colour mean?

Take the pupils' suggestions.

Jesus told his disciples that everyone who asked for something from God would get an answer, but it wouldn't always be an immediate green light for 'go'. Sometimes they might have to wait for a while, like waiting at an amber light. At other times they might have to stop and wait for longer, like waiting at a red light. And Jesus said that God would never give people things that were bad for them.

The disciples had watched Jesus pray. They realised that Jesus had the power to talk to God and they hoped he had the power to teach them too. *Refer back to the three words.* He told them that they should tell God they love him, ask him for their needs and say sorry for the things they had done to hurt him. He would always hear them, even if it seemed like they had to wait for a while.

The Bible says that we can pray to God in the same way that Jesus taught his disciples. It says that when we talk to God today, he still hears us and will still answer us.

Optional prayer time:

Give thanks to God that we can still talk to him today. Ask him to help us talk to him more, to tell him we love him, to ask for his help and to say sorry.

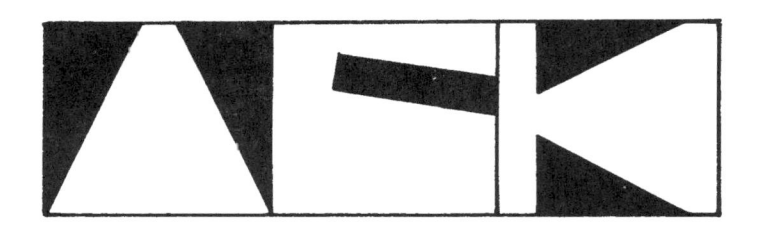

Solution: LOVE ASK SORRY

What did his friends think?

5.1

―――――― *Bible base: Luke 10:38–42* ――――――

Teaching objectives:

To show that Christians believe Jesus wants us to get to know him better and wants us to be his friend. The Bible says that this is more important than anything else.

You will need:

- In advance, put together a pop quiz based on current songs being listened to by primary school children. You can find this out from any pop music magazine, listening to the charts, on the Internet at www.bbc.co.uk/totp, or by looking at the most recent pop compilation CD. Either play a snippet of a song and ask the children to name the title and the band, or give the pupils the name of a band and ask them to name their current hit. Be sure to check titles and lyrics carefully in advance for swearing and appropriateness!
- Acetates or posters of the words 'What did his friends think?' and 'What do you think?'

Introductory activity:

Conduct your pop quiz.

How do they know the answers to this quiz? They listen to music. Why do they listen to music? Because they like it and they think it's worth it.

Optional extra activity: invite about eight pupils to come to the front, divide them into two teams and put them at either side of a line in the centre of the assembly hall. Give each team a supply of paper balls made out of newspaper and allow them one minute to throw as many as they can into the other team's area. They can pick up balls thrown by the opposition and fire them back over the line. Encourage the rest of the assembly to cheer for their side.

Make the point that they were all very busy for a minute, but the best way of winning would have been to save the newspaper balls at their own side until a couple of seconds before the end. Then they wouldn't have been so busy and would also have achieved a better result.

Display the acetate or poster, 'What did his friends think?'

Today's story is about someone called Mary. Mary may have liked listening to music too, but there was something the Bible says she really enjoyed doing, and that was listening to Jesus. He told fantastic stories and was always interested in people.

When you hear the name 'Mary', be very quiet and put your finger to your lips.

Mary had a sister called Martha, and while Martha enjoyed listening to Jesus too, she thought it was really important to make nice food for him and offer him a comfortable home to visit. Sometimes she was so busy doing this that she didn't have time to stop and listen to Jesus.

When you hear the name 'Martha', we are all going to do different things, because she was so busy!

Divide the assembly into four.

Group 1: Mime cooking
Group 2: Mime cleaning
Group 3: Mime setting the table
Group 4: Mime washing up

On the occasion we are thinking about today, Jesus had gone to visit his two friends, **Mary** and **Martha**. As usual, they were both delighted to see him, and **Mary** sat down at his feet to listen to the stories of where he had been and what he had been doing. **Martha** was delighted to see him too, but she was worried about what the house looked like and what they would eat for their dinner. So while **Mary** sat at Jesus' feet, **Martha** rushed around, cooking and cleaning and setting the table and washing the dishes. **Martha** was exhausted!

Eventually, **Martha** went to Jesus and complained.

'Jesus,' she moaned, 'don't you think it's unfair that I'm doing all the work while **Mary** sits and does nothing to help me?'

But Jesus spoke gently to **Martha**, who was still thinking about all the things she had to do, and told her that actually, **Mary** had got it right. **Mary** was doing the most important thing – listening to him – and that was really how to please him.

Tell the pupils that you have finished the story, so they should stop doing the actions when they hear 'Martha' or 'Mary'. What did Jesus' friends think? They both wanted to please him, but Martha had got the wrong idea. She was worried about lots of unimportant things, like how the house looked and making him the best meal ever, whereas Mary had chosen to do something much more valuable: she was listening to what he said.

Display the acetate or poster, 'What do you think?'

What would you have thought if you had been there? Would you have been like Martha, too busy doing other things to spend time with Jesus, or would you have been like Mary, eager to hear all that he had to say?

Christians believe that the most important thing for anyone to do is to get to know Jesus better by reading the Bible and praying, but sometimes people are too busy doing other things.

> **Optional prayer time:**
>
> Give thanks that Jesus is more interested in us than in what we do. Pray that each of us might get to know him better.

What did the businessman think?

5.2

——— *Bible base: Luke 19:1–10* ———

Teaching objectives:

To show that the Bible says Jesus cared about people whom no one else liked.

You will need:

- A newspaper listing 'executive' jobs which offer nice perks.
- Acetates or posters of the words 'What did the businessman think?' and 'What do you think?'
- A large card with the word 'WINNER' on it, plus a 'D' and an 'S' to go over the 'W' to spell DINNER and SINNER.
- A few pieces of broadsheet newspaper, cut into two along the middle and taped together to make a long strip of newspaper. Fold this strip concertina-style so that each section is roughly A4 in size.

Introductory activity:

Show the assembly some advertisements for executive jobs. What sort of special extras are they offering? Read out some examples. Ask the pupils to raise their hand if these would encourage them to apply for the job.

The things we read about in the advertisements would all be very nice in a job, but would they be enough to make someone happy?

Take the folded piece of newspaper and begin to cut it into the shape of a person, being sure to go right out to the edges with the arms and legs. (Practise this activity in advance to be sure that you end up with a paper chain of people!) As you do so, ask the following question:

What would be the most important thing that you would look for in a job? *Take some suggestions, eg good salary, good holidays. When you have finished cutting out the shape of a person, ask two volunteers to come out and hold either end of the chain of people.*

All of us need friends, and no matter how good a job might be, it is no substitute for knowing people who care for us.

Display acetate or poster, 'What did the businessman think?'

Today's story from the Bible is about a man who was a very successful businessman with a very important job. He worked for the government, collecting the money that people owed: their taxes. The man's name was Zacchaeus, and he lived a long time before there were cars or foreign holidays, but one of the benefits he did enjoy in his job was that he could take as much money as he liked from people. So, if I owed the government £1, he could ask me for £2 and pocket the difference. Or if I owed £5, he could ask me for £10. As you can imagine, Zacchaeus was soon a very rich man!

In terms of business success, Zacchaeus was definitely a WINNER.

Ask a pupil to come to the front to hold up the WINNER card.

In other ways, however, Zacchaeus was not doing so well. Let's imagine that our chain of newspaper people represents the people who he collected money from. What do you think they thought of him? *Take some suggestions, eg he was greedy, he was selfish.*

People hated him because he had become rich from taking their money. In their opinion, he did things wrong, he was not a WINNER, he was a SINNER *(stick 'S' over 'W' of WINNER)*. 'Sinner' is a word that the Bible uses to describe someone who is not perfect and has done things that are wrong.

So Zacchaeus was very rich but he was also very dishonest and very lonely.

One day, however, something happened to change Zacchaeus' life for ever – he met Jesus. Jesus was visiting Jericho, where Zacchaeus lived, but there were so many people, and Zacchaeus was so short, that he could not see over people's heads.

For fun, you could go behind the chain of newspaper people and crouch behind it, pretending to try to see over their heads.

As you can imagine, people were not too keen to let Zacchaeus the SINNER through, this man who took all their money. And so poor Zacchaeus was stuck at the back of the crowd.

Suddenly, he had an idea. *Come around to the front of the chain again.* He ran ahead of the crowds and climbed a tree at the side of the road, hiding in the branches so that no one could see him. And there he waited, hoping to catch a glimpse of Jesus and to hear what he was saying as he passed by.

Soon, Jesus was right underneath Zacchaeus and, much to his surprise, he looked up to where Zacchaeus was hiding and asked him to come down and take him to his house for DINNER *(stick the 'D' over the 'S' of SINNER).*

Zacchaeus was amazed! No one usually spoke to him and no one had ever asked to come to his house for tea!

The crowds, however, were annoyed. 'That man is a SINNER!' they muttered *(reveal the word SINNER again).*

Zacchaeus was too delighted to care about what they were saying and he rushed off to prepare the DINNER *(replace the 'D').* And after DINNER, Zacchaeus did something amazing. He gave away half of his money to the poor and paid back four times any money that he had taken unfairly.

Zacchaeus had changed by spending time with Jesus. Christians believe that when we're sorry for what we've done wrong, God can change us from sinners to winners, as he did with Zacchaeus. Uncover the original word, WINNER.

Display the acetate or poster, 'What do you think?'

What would you have thought if you were there? Would you have thought that Zacchaeus was too bad to spend time with Jesus? Or would you have been like Zacchaeus, wanting to be with Jesus?

> **Optional prayer time:**
>
> Give thanks that Jesus can change people, not just on the surface but deep inside. He can change them from sinners into winners!

What did the criminals think?

5.3

──────── *Bible base: Luke 23:32–43* ────────

Teaching objectives:

To introduce pupils to two people who looked at the evidence they had in order to work out who Jesus was.

You will need:

- Pictures of celebrities, preferably in unlikely locations or in some way disguised, either photocopied on to acetate or poster-size, cut into four or five pieces.
- 'YES' and 'NO' visuals from pages 110 and 111, copied on to acetates or posters and cut into jigsaw pieces.
- Acetates or posters of the words 'What did the criminals think?' and 'What do you think?'

Introductory activity:

Show the assembly the pictures of celebrities, one piece at a time, asking them to raise their hand as soon as they think they know who it is.

Some people here were able to recognise these celebrities even though they couldn't see the whole picture *(and, if this is the case, in an unexpected place)*. Other pupils found it much harder to see who it was.

In the Bible, some people saw Jesus doing amazing miracles and they thought that he was someone very special. Other people saw him teaching crowds of people and they thought he was someone very wise.

Christians believe that Jesus was the Son of God. As the Son of

God, they believed he could do amazing things. I'm sure a lot of people were surprised when this person whom they believed to be so powerful was put to death on a cross.

Display the acetate or poster, 'What did the criminals think?'

The Bible says that two criminals were crucified next to Jesus. The first criminal definitely did not think Jesus was the Son of God. He mocked Jesus and made fun of him, telling him to do one last miracle and save them all from death. He didn't understand who Jesus was.

The second criminal recognised Jesus as someone very special. He knew Jesus was different from anyone else he had ever met. He knew that Jesus was completely innocent, yet had not argued with the judge when he was condemned to death.

As they were dying, the second criminal asked Jesus to remember him when he went to his kingdom. He believed that Jesus was the Son of God and that when he died, he would be going to God's kingdom in heaven.

We put together the pieces of the jigsaws to work out who the celebrities were. Both these men had pieced together the evidence they saw but they had come up with different answers. Was Jesus the Son of God?

The first criminal saw the following evidence:

Put together the pieces of the jigsaw saying 'NO' as you explain what evidence he saw.

He was **beaten** by the soldiers as though he were a criminal.
He was being **punished**, so he must have done something wrong.
He was **bleeding** and suffering like a normal human being.
He was **dying** – how could the Son of God die?
He was **weak** – how could people believe that he was a mighty king?
People **made fun of** him – he seemed a bit pathetic.

The first criminal did not think that Jesus could possibly be the Son of God.

The second criminal, however, saw different evidence:

Put together the pieces of the jigsaw saying 'YES' as you explain what evidence he saw.

He was **innocent** – this man had done nothing wrong.

He was **amazing** – he had helped people and yet when they were punishing him he did not fight back.
He was **trustworthy** – he had never let anyone down in his life.
He was **pure** – he still cared about people around him even when he was dying.
He was **peaceful** – he didn't seem scared.
He was **hopeful** – he believed that death was not going to be the end.

Although he was dying, there was something different about Jesus, and the second criminal believed that yes, Jesus was the Son of God.

Display the acetate or poster, 'What do you think?'

The Bible says that both these criminals looked at what they knew about Jesus and decided what they thought about him. Think about what you know about Jesus. What sort of things did he do and say? Do you think he was someone you would have liked to know?

> **Optional prayer time:**
>
> Ask the pupils to think for a few moments about what they know about Jesus. Then say a short, general prayer thanking God for all the things they have thought of that they know about him.

Peaceful Hopeful

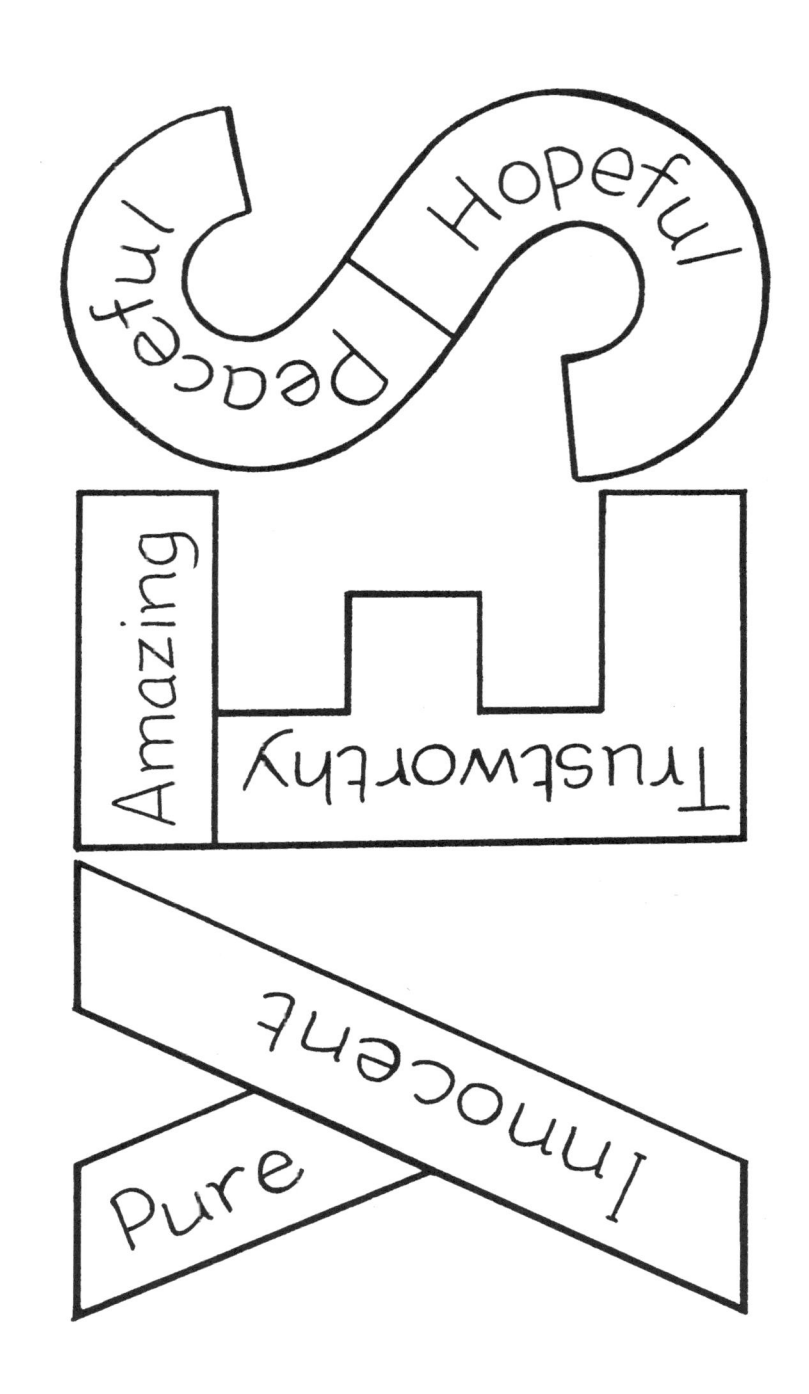

Amazing Trustworthy

Innocent Pure

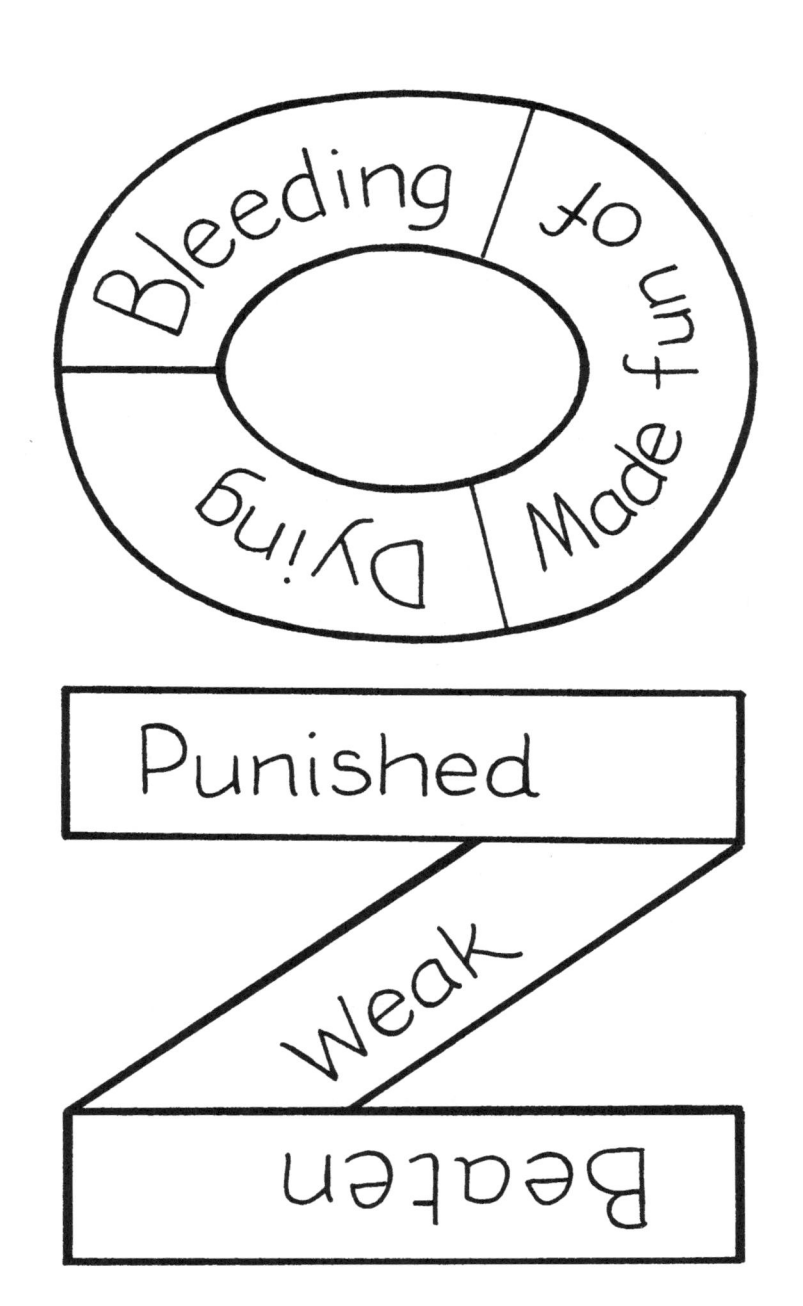

Bleeding • Made fun of • Dying • Punished • Weak • Beaten

What did the fisherman think?

5.4

---Bible base: Luke 5:1–11---

Teaching objectives:

To show that the Bible says Jesus accepts people who are keen to follow him, no matter what they are like.

> **You will need:**
> - Props for introductory activity:
> - Chef – apron, mixing bowl, a few small packets of baking products, a spoon.
> - Nursery teacher – storybook, paints and brushes.
> - Driving instructor – car keys, a map.
> - Cue cards with the following information:
>   'You really want to be a chef! You do not know how to cook. You have never cooked or worn an apron before. Put on the apron upside down and put all the packets in the bowl without opening them.'
>   'You really want to be a nursery teacher! You cannot read and you hate getting messy. Open the book upside down and refuse to touch the paints.'
>   'You really want to be a driving instructor! You have never driven (you are too young!). You do not know what the car keys are for, and you think a map is a funny picture.'
> - Acetates or posters with the words, 'What did the fisherman think?' and 'What do you think?'

Introductory activity:

Ask a member of staff to help you choose three pupils in advance with some dramatic ability and explain that you are going to interview each one of them for a different job. Tell them that they should pretend to be really keen to do the job. Explain that the interview will involve them being given some objects relating to that job, but they should pretend to have no idea what to do with them. Reassure them that they only have to answer your questions and give them the cue cards.

Today we are going to have some job interviews in the assembly.

Ask the enthusiastic job hunters to come forward.

Pupil one wants to be a chef. Instead of an interview, we will give them a practical test.

Do you want to be a chef? Do you really want to be a chef?

Give them the apron and ask them to put it on.

Have you ever worn an apron before?

Give them the bowl, spoon and food packets.

Have you ever cooked before?

I know you are really keen to get the job but you really need to get some more experience before you can be a chef.

Pupil two wants to be a nursery teacher.

Do you want to be a nursery teacher? Do you really want to be a nursery teacher?

Give them the book and ask them to read a story to the assembly.

Have you ever read a book before?

Give them the paints.

Do you know how to paint?

I know you are really keen to be a nursery teacher, but you need to be able to read to teach young children! And you certainly will have to be happy to get messy!

Pupil three wants to be a driving instructor.

Do you want to be a driving instructor? Do you really want to be a driving instructor?

Give them the keys.

Do you know what these are?

Give them the map.

Do you know what this is? Have you ever driven before? What age are you?

I know you really want to be a driving instructor, but you have to be able to drive first, and you need to be a lot older.

Thank the pupils for their help and ask them to take their seats again.

To get any job, you need to have the right skills. It is not enough to be really keen to do a job – you need to be qualified. However, there is one job you don't need special skills to do. You just need to be keen.

We are going to hear about someone today who had a job he was very well qualified to do. The Bible tells us that this man was a fisherman and his name was Simon Peter. He was a very good fisherman and was happy doing his job until one day he met Jesus and everything changed.

Display the acetate or poster, 'What did the fisherman think?'

Simon Peter was a fisherman in a very hot country, which meant that he went out fishing at night when it was cooler and the fish came up to the surface of the water. One morning, after a hard night when they had caught nothing, Simon Peter and his friends were cleaning their nets. They saw Jesus on the shore, teaching a huge crowd of people. They had seen Jesus before and had heard some of the things he was saying, and so, as they worked, they listened to his amazing stories about God.

Soon, though, the crowd was so huge that lots of people could not hear what he was saying. Jesus came and asked Simon Peter if he would take him out a little way on to the water in his boat. Once he was out on the water, people would see him better, and as his voice carried over the water, they would hear him better too. Simon Peter and his friends were tired, but they didn't like to say no, so they agreed and pushed out from the shore.

After a while, when Jesus had finished talking to the crowd, he told Simon Peter and his friends to take the boat out again into the deep water and let down the nets for a catch. Now, Jesus may well have been a great teacher who knew lots about God, but Simon Peter was the fisherman, and he knew that in the middle of the day, when the sun was hot, they would never catch any fish. But, because it was Jesus who told him to do it, he decided he would, even though he had just finished cleaning all the nets. There was something about this man Jesus – he seemed to know what he was talking about!

So out they went, down went the nets and everyone waited. And waited. Suddenly, there was a huge tug on the nets, and it felt as if the whole boat might tip over! There were so many fish that Simon Peter and his friends needed to call some other fishermen from another boat to come and help them to pull the nets aboard.

What was Simon Peter's reaction? He was amazed and knew then that Jesus was someone totally different from anyone he had ever met before. He fell at his feet, asking him to go away, not because he didn't like him, but because he did not feel that he was good enough to be with someone like Jesus!

But Jesus did not go away. In fact, Jesus called him to be his follower. Simon Peter had shown the qualification he needed to start his new 'job' as a follower of Jesus! He really wanted to be Jesus' follower, but he needed to recognise how different from Jesus he was and how he needed Jesus' help to become more like Jesus. *Display the acetate or poster,* 'What do you think?'

What would you have thought if you had been there? Would you have felt that Jesus was too amazing for you to be around?

Christians believe that the qualifications are still the same for people to become Jesus' followers. They simply need to realise that they are not good enough to be Jesus' followers, but if they are keen to follow him, he will still accept them and help them.

Optional prayer time:

Give thanks that Jesus is not expecting us to be perfect people, but he wants us to be honest people. Thank him that we can all meet his qualifications to be his follower, if we want to, and if we admit that we are not good enough.

What did the follower think?

5.5

――――――― *Bible base: Luke 9:18–20* ―――――――

Teaching objectives:

To discover what Jesus' followers thought about him and to encourage pupils to think for themselves about their own opinions about him.

You will need:
- Flip chart and pen.
- Acetates or posters with the words: 'What did the follower think?' and 'What do you think?'
- Acetates or posters with the words: 'Who do people say that I am?' and 'Who do you say that I am?'

Introductory activity:

Ask the pupils who their favourite band or singer is. Take some suggestions. Choose two pupils who like very different groups/singers to come to the front.

Write the names of the two bands at the top of the flip chart sheet and draw a line down the middle dividing the sheet into two columns.

Ask the first pupil to think of three words that describe what they think of their favourite band. Write the words on the sheet under the name of their band.

Ask the second pupil to think of three words that describe what they think of their favourite band and write these words in the other column.

117

Now ask each pupil in turn to think of three words they would use to describe the other person's favourite band (if you think it is necessary, make it clear that while they can say that they do not like the band, they should not say anything rude).

There should now be two very different views of each band being expressed on the sheet! Ask each pupil which views they think are more important for us to remember – their own or those of the other person?

Thank the pupils and ask them to take their seats.

Optional extra activity: spend some time discussing with the pupils what sort of things people follow, eg football teams, a sport, a TV programme, etc. How do they show that they are a fan? (eg wearing a football strip, going to matches, buying the videos or DVDs.)

When we are followers of a band (or a football team, or a TV programme) we think our own ideas about them are right and are more important than anyone else's view. If I were to get confused and muddle up the opinions of our two volunteers (*use their names*) they would not be very happy!

Display the acetate or poster, 'What did the follower think?'

Jesus had followers too, called disciples. The Bible says that one day, Jesus asked his disciples two questions to find out what people thought about him.

The first question Jesus asked the disciples was what other people thought of him. *Show the acetate:* 'Who do people say that I am?'

Well, people had lots of different opinions! They had seen all the amazing things that he was doing and knew that he was someone special, but they had lots of weird ideas! Some people thought he was his cousin, John the Baptist, come back to life, and others thought he was a famous religious leader from centuries before come back to life.

But then Jesus asked them a second question. *Show them the second acetate:* 'Who do you say that I am?'

Which answer do you think was more important to him – what strangers thought or what his closest friends thought? *Take suggestions from the pupils.*

Simon Peter answered straight away. 'You are the Messiah, sent from God.'

Simon Peter had been an ordinary fisherman until Jesus called him; then he had become one of Jesus' closest followers and friends. As he saw all that Jesus did and said, he decided that this man was sent from God. Simon Peter called Jesus the 'Messiah', which was a name people used to describe the special person that God was going to send to them to set them free from their enemies. *Display the acetate or poster,* 'What do you think?'

I wonder what we would have said if we had known Jesus and had seen all the amazing things that he did? It is easy to answer the first question, as there are so many different opinions about who Jesus is. Some people say that he was just a nice man and a good teacher, others say that he was no one special, some even claim that he never existed. Yet the Bible says, and millions of people believe, that Jesus is who he claimed to be: the 'Messiah', the special person sent by God.

> **Optional prayer time:**
>
> Give thanks that Jesus is interested in each individual and in what they think about him. Pray that each of us could find out more about him.

What did the officer think?

5.6

———— *Bible base: Luke 7:1–10* ————

Teaching objectives:

To introduce pupils to someone powerful in the Bible who recognised that Jesus was also a powerful person.

You will need:

- Cards with the following words written on them:
  Set 1: 'pop band', 'Prime Minister', 'head teacher', 'officer', 'football manager'.
  Set 2: 'fans', 'Britain', 'school', 'soldiers', 'football team'.
- Picture from page 124 photocopied on to acetate or card.
- Acetates or posters of the words 'What did the officer think?' and 'What do you think?'

Introductory activity:

Invite two pupils to come to the front and give one the first set of cards described above and the other the second set.

Who has power over what? As pupil one holds up their 'person' card, the rest of the assembly should choose which of pupil two's cards they have power over.

Choose one or two of the people mentioned on the card, eg the Prime Minister, an officer.

How could these people show their power over others? For example, what decisions can a football manager make for his team? (eg who is going to play in a match, what position each person plays, when they will have training, etc.)

To develop the idea of authority, play a game of 'Simon says'. Give the assembly various instructions, for example, 'Simon says touch your nose', 'Simon says clap your hands', etc. Pupils should do exactly as you say so long as the instruction is preceded by 'Simon says'. You may wish to bring some pupils to the front to help you spot others who get it wrong.

Because you all know the rules of the game, you know that you must obey whatever 'Simon' tells you to do. In today's Bible story we will meet someone who had authority to tell people what to do.

Display the acetate or poster, 'What did the officer think?'

Today's story is about an army officer. An officer has authority over his soldiers. He could tell them what to do and could make decisions for them. If you were all soldiers and I was your officer, you would have to do exactly what I said. And because this officer was quite important, he also had lots of servants to look after him. In this story we will meet one of them.

Choose six pupils to be servants and ask them to come to the front. The last pupil to mime each of the following orders as you call them out is eliminated until only one pupil remains:

Scrub the floor
Polish my shoes
Wash the dishes
Stand up straight
Bring me a chair
Vacuum the carpet

(You may wish to add in one or two other commands as a 'warm up'.) Ask the pupils to sit down again.

Show the picture from page 124.

An officer could tell his servants to do anything he liked – they were more like slaves.

Even though the servants had to do everything the officer told them to do, some things were still out of his control. The servant in our story became ill and was close to death, and no matter how many times the officer told him to get better, he couldn't obey.

We can't get rid of illness just by telling it to go away! What could the officer do? Think of some possibilities *(eg he could get some medicine, he could call a doctor, he could give him some time off work).* I imagine he tried all these things, but no one and nothing seemed to be able to help – the servant was dying.

The officer did believe there was still one more person he hadn't tried who might be able to help – Jesus. Jesus was not a doctor, but the officer had heard some amazing stories about some of the things that Jesus had done. *(If you have been doing a series on stories from Luke's Gospel, you may wish to re-cap here and find out what pupils remember about previous assemblies.)*

The officer knew that he had power over people to tell them what to do, but he believed that Jesus had power over more than just people – he had power over illness too.

In fact, the officer had so much faith in Jesus that he believed he could help his servant without even being there! The officer's friends told Jesus that the officer believed that if Jesus just said the word, his servant would get better! And that is what happened. Jesus never actually went to the officer's home or met the servant.

Show the picture.

The Bible says the servant was completely healed! When we played 'Simon says', I asked you to do very simple tasks and you did them. But Jesus ordered an illness to go away from someone whom he had never even met and it did!

What do you think the army officer thought? The officer was a very important man, who gave orders to people and knew that they would obey him. In Jesus the officer saw someone who could control things the officer couldn't even dream of controlling. He believed that Jesus could help his servant.

Display the acetate or poster, 'What do you think?'

What do you think you would have thought if you had been there? It would have been strange to see someone so ill getting well just because someone told them to! Do you think you would have been amazed?

> **Optional prayer time:**
>
> Pray that we would discover more about Jesus and the amazing things that he did.

Meanwhile.....

What did Mary think?

5.7

——— Bible base: Luke 7:36–50 ———

Teaching objectives:

To show that the Bible says Jesus does not judge by appearances but accepts anyone who genuinely comes to him because they love him.

You will need:

- The following objects wrapped up separately to look like gifts:
  a bar of chocolate
  a large box with some rubbish in it
  a sweet.
- A piece of wrapping paper with a £5 note inside, scrunched up into a ball.
- Two acetates or posters with the words, 'What did Mary think?' and 'What do you think?'
- Another large cardboard box covered in expensive-looking paper.
- A small matchbox with two pieces of paper inside saying: 'Mary wept at Jesus' feet', 'Mary poured perfume on Jesus' feet'.
- The following phrases written on separate pieces of card: 'Simon invited Jesus for dinner', 'Simon was religious', 'Simon did good things', 'Simon was well-liked'.

Introductory activity:

Choose a volunteer to come to the front and show them the three parcels and the piece of wrapping paper. You may wish to say that they are presents left over from your birthday or from Christmas if doing the assembly in January.

Explain that they can have one of the four items. Allow them to pick them up and rattle or squeeze them, but not open them. As they are doing that, ask the rest of the assembly which one they would choose. Ask the volunteer for their decision.

When they have opened their chosen present, reveal the contents of the other three (if they have not picked the bar of chocolate, it might be nice to give it to them at the end to thank them for their help, if the head teacher agrees).

Most of us judged these presents by their appearance. Not many people would choose an old piece of paper instead of the big box or a bar of chocolate, but actually, it was not what it seemed on the outside. It was actually something special.

Today's story in the Bible is about someone who did not seem very special, but who had something very special to offer to Jesus. In today's story, Jesus met two people.

The first person he met was called Simon, and he was very rich and important.

Show the pupils the large expensive-looking box.

Let's imagine that this box represents all the good things Simon has ever done. Clearly he was quite a good person!

Start to stick the cards about Simon on the box while you explain what sort of a person he was.

Simon was a religious man. He was a Pharisee, which meant that he was quite an important person. He did good things and was well-liked by the people. He had invited Jesus for dinner. Sounds like a pretty good guy!

However, while Jesus was at his house for dinner, someone else arrived. The Bible isn't clear about what her name was, but some people think she was called Mary, so that's what we will call her. *Show the matchbox to the assembly.*

Let's imagine that the matchbox represents all the good things Mary has done. It doesn't look very impressive!

People described her as a 'sinful woman', meaning that she did a lot of things that were wrong.

She couldn't offer Jesus a nice meal. People didn't think she was a very nice person.

But Mary did offer Jesus something very special.

Open the matchbox. Take out and read the two pieces of paper inside ('Mary wept at Jesus' feet', 'Mary poured perfume on Jesus' feet').

That sounds a bit strange to us, but in those days it would have been a sign of great respect and love, and would have been a welcome treat for hot, tired feet!

When Simon saw what was happening, he was very surprised. 'If Jesus were really sent from God, he would know what sort of a woman this is and he wouldn't let her touch him,' thought Simon.

Jesus, however, did not tell the woman to go away. It did not seem like she had much to offer, but Jesus did not just look on the outside. He was interested in what was really in a person's heart. He knew that Mary was weeping and pouring perfume on his feet because she loved him. He showed that he loved her by accepting her gift.

Display the acetate or poster, 'What did Mary think?'

Mary thought that Jesus was someone special, and although she didn't have much to offer, she wanted Jesus to know she loved him.

Display the acetate or poster, 'What do you think?'

What would you have thought if you had been there? Would you have thought that what Mary did was strange?

> **Optional prayer time:**
>
> Give thanks that Jesus does not judge by appearances, but came to earth to show his love to all people.

Another great resource from Scripture Union...

Ready-made assemblies about famous people
Tony Dobinson

Twenty-four instant assembly outlines suitable for use in both junior and lower secondary schools.

Focusing on the exciting true life stories of famous Christians around the world, the assemblies also contain:

- Challenging introductions based on contemporary situations
- Times of reflection
- 'Bible bits'
- Prayer suggestions
- Quiz questions

The assemblies are grouped into five main sections: Creation and Identity, Freedom, Justice, Hope and Forgiveness. An invaluable subject-link index enables quick and easy preparation of an assembly relevant to a particular theme.

All the material you need to prepare an attention-grabbing, challenging assembly with the minimum of fuss and time!

ISBN 1 85999 300 1

*You can buy this book at your local Christian bookshop, or online at www.scriptureunion.org.uk/publishing
or call Mail Order direct
01908 856006*